Take Charge of Your Life

Patricia Diane Cota-Robles

The New Age Study of Humanity's Purpose, Inc.
P.O. Box 41883
Tucson, Arizona 85717

First printing August 15, 1984
Second printing August 15, 1985
Third printing December 31, 1986
Manufactured in the United States of America

Library of Congress Cataloging in Publication Data
TXU 140-139

ISBN 0-9615287-0-2

First Edition

Suggested Reading List and Tape List: p. 163

TAKE CHARGE OF YOUR LIFE
By Patricia Diane Cota-Robles

REVIEWS AND COMMENTS ABOUT
TAKE CHARGE OF YOUR LIFE

In the past several years bookstores have begun to burgeon with volumes suggesting every imaginable path to heightened awareness. Beneficial spiritual transformation seems to be the subject of the times, and publishers are happily obliging our quest for personal growth.

TAKE CHARGE OF YOUR LIFE is a lucid and well organized smorgasbord of useful information intended to help you: "Witness a natural unfolding of your highest potential that will bring inner peace, calm, harmony, control and success into your life that is beyond your greatest expectation." Author Patricia Cota-Robles set quite a task for herself, and the result is surprisingly effective. She has managed to bring "spiritual self-help" books to a refreshingly informative and readable new level.

Seeds of Peace

Patricia,

A special thanks for sharing your very positive, very spiritual work with me. The world and all of us in it will be better for your loving efforts.

Continue living in love and sharing your warmth and specialness with the many in need.

Leo Buscaglia

Patricia,

Jan and I have read your book–and oh my! The energy was incredible!!! We love you so much!

John Randolph Price
The Quartus Foundation For Spiritual Research, Inc.

Patricia,

"The book is just excellent. What we have seen so far tells us a great deal. In our opinion, it may well be the most practical manual to the transformation of consciousness that has yet been published."

Bob & Edith Helm–Peace The 21st

Patricia,

My brief perusal shows me the sincerity of your commitment to serve. I wonder at the great variety of ways that are part of this great birth and I am thankful.

In growing Love,
Richard Moss, MD

Patricia,

Many thanks for your beautiful book. We were glad to know of the positive work you are doing in the U.S. to further right human relations and an understanding of spirituality in daily life.

Yours in Companionship,
Rudolph Schneider
Alice Boainain

"The New Age Study of Humanity's Purpose offers an excellent book entitled *Take Charge of Your Life*. The material is elegant in its simplicity, well-presented, and easy to understand; and is suitable for anyone who aspires to higher consciousness."

Peace The 21st – Toronto, Ontario, Canada

Patricia,

Thank you for your wonderfully inspiring book. We share your work and mission.

S. Rickert Grace
Unity School of Christianity
Unity Village, Missouri

Patricia,

Thank you kindly for your recent book. It is marvelous to watch how ideas like this can spread across the world, through the networks.

We have made your book available to the group here in London.

Richard Bryant-Jefferies
for WORLD GOODWILL, London U.K.

Patricia,

Thank you for the wonderful gift of your book. Not only have I enjoyed it, but I have asked our bookstore manager to keep it in stock. I have given it, as a result, to quite a number of students or seekers on the inner path when I feel they are really ready to take action in their lives.

With Every Blessing,
Rev. LeRoy E. Zemke

Patricia,

Thank you for the book. I treasure it.

Andrea Kay Smith, Director
Partnerships In Peace, Inc.

Recommended Book of the Month –

This excellent book covers many topics that Quartus members have inquired about, including The Power of Thought; Self-Awareness, the Key to Self-Mastery; Attaining Goals Through Creative Visualization; Transforming Your Relationships Through the Power of Unconditional Love; The Secret of Financial Freedom; Healing and Maintaining the Health of Your Physical Body; The Mysterious Chakras; The Use of Color to Help You Reach Your Highest Potential; Music and Harmony; and We Are on the Dawn of a New Age!

The Quartus Report

Dedication

This book is lovingly dedicated to every man, woman and child on this Planet who is anxiously awaiting the opportunity to burst the bonds of poverty, sickness, loneliness, stress, failure, doubt, fear and limitation and soar to the heights of their full potential through ILLUMINED TRUTH, SELF-MASTERY, VIBRANT HEALTH, PEACE OF MIND, FAMILY CONTENTMENT, PROSPERITY, SUCCESS AND ABOUND-ING JOY.

YOUR OPPORTUNITY IS AT HAND!

Acknowledgments

My Heartfelt Love and Gratitude to:

My Husband, the sweetest most loving man I have ever known, for his endless support and encouragement;

My Son and Daughter for their Wisdom and the Joy they are adding to my Life;

My Mother and Father for the learning experiences they afforded me and for allowing me entrance into the physical plane through them;

My Sister and my two Brothers for keeping me ever humble;

My dear friend Kay Meyer for her commitment, her selfless service to the Light and her hours and hours of typing and re-typing;

Anna Cota-Robles for her artistic abilities and the beautiful cover she designed and illustrated from a concept by my son Joao;

Alice Burns for her kindness, her faith and her courage;

All the rest of my family, friends and co-workers for their tolerance, love and understanding.

Introduction

Every single person on this Planet is special and unique: you, your friends, loved ones, co-workers, and associates. Every person you know has gifts, talents, qualities and abilities that no one else on this entire Earth possesses in exactly the same way.

The majority of people are continually looking outside of themselves for people they can look up to and admire. What I want you to do is look inside, into your very own heart, and when you do, you will find one of the most beautiful, gifted, exceptional people you would ever want to meet.

Because of a lack of understanding, people have allowed themselves to be engulfed in a myriad of negative circumstances. Consequently, most people are struggling so hard just to survive that they haven't been able to recognize their full potential. Regardless of how inadequate you feel or what self-destructive, self-defeating behavior you might have programmed into yourself, you have a super-conscious mind that is continually prompting and prodding you on to reach your highest potential. Once you truly understand the natural laws that govern all of us and apply the very tangible, practical tools that are available to you, you will be able to clear away the things that have been preventing you from seeing how special you really are, and you will witness a natural unfolding of your highest potential that will bring an inner peace, calm, harmony, control and SUCCESS into your life that is beyond your greatest expectation.

You have the ability to turn your life around. The statement "Today is the first day of the rest of your life" can be a reality for you. All you need to do is to have the courage to experiment for yourself and apply the information that is presented in this book. You have more support than you could possibly know. The time to take charge of your life is *now*.

Every tenet that I have written about in this book I have applied, experimented with and proved to myself to be true. In my quest for knowledge I came across many more theories, but if, after careful application, they didn't work for me, I discarded them. This is not to say they weren't true, but if I am unable to prove something to myself I will not teach it to others.

Even though I totally accept as truth what I have written in the pages of this book, I do not want you to just take my word for it. My hope is that you will trust me enough to accept this information as a possibility and experiment with it yourself. Apply it to your life and marvel at the transformation that will take place.

Table of Contents

1

You Can Take Charge of Your Life

The key to self-mastery is self-awareness. In order for you to begin creating what you really want in your life, you must first determine how your life got into its present state of disarray.

This universe is governed by natural laws and all humanity is subject to them. The natural law that creates what is going on in our lives is called The Law of the Circle. This Law is scientific and as accurate as the laws of gravity, physics, mathematics, or music. Throughout the history of the world, The Law of the Circle has been presented to mankind in various ways. The basic principle of this law is, simply, WHAT WE SEND OUT THROUGH OUR THOUGHTS, WORDS, ACTIONS AND FEELINGS RETURNS TO US.

In ancient philosophies this law was referred to as karma or the Law of Cause and Effect. In Judaism it is referred to as *reaping what we sow* or *an eye for an eye and a tooth for a tooth*. In Christianity it is referred to as *casting our bread upon the water and having it return to us*. Now, in more scientific terminology, this same law is referred to as *like attracts like*, *action and reaction*, or *radiation and magnetization*.

We have been told since the beginning of time that we are all subject to this law whether we believe in it or not, just as we are all subject to the law of gravity. If you jump off a roof and you don't believe in the law of gravity, it isn't going to make any difference. You're going to hit the ground just the same.

Even though our belief doesn't affect the accuracy of the law, our belief can cause us to make mistakes that will catapult us into the pits of chaos and confusion. If you strive to understand and apply the scientific principles of The Law of the Circle, I assure you that you will truly become the master of your life and save yourself a great deal of frustration, sadness, and pain.

By observing what is going on in the world at the present time, as well as the circumstances of our own individual lives, it may seem as though we are living in rampant chaos beyond our control. If we were to take things at face value it would be very easy for us to throw our hands up in despair and say, "What's the use?" But fortunately a unique paradox is occurring at the present time. On the one hand people are feeling anxious and uneasy about their personal lives and the overall world situation, but on the other hand there is a welling up of hope in their hearts, an inner knowledge that they have the ability to improve the quality of their lives. There are more self-help groups, motivational seminars, physical fitness centers and self-awareness classes springing up across the country than ever before.

It seems as though people are allowing pain to be their motivator. As long as we are comfortable we usually don't put forth any extra effort to improve our lives. We often wait until we are in the pits of despair before we begin looking for a better way, because human beings are creatures of habit. As long as we are healthy we may not give our bodies a second thought, but as soon as we get sick, this becomes a major issue in our lives. As long as we are financially secure, money may be taken for granted, but if we lose our job or run into financial difficulty, then we have a real problem. Our family life can run on status quo for years with very little attention, but if a spouse decides to leave or our children go astray, then we begin to scramble around frantically trying to recapture what we allowed to slip away. If this is the case in your life, you are certainly not alone. It is precisely because of the current chaos on the planet that people are desperately searching for a better way of life.

The principles I am sharing with you in this book have literally transformed my life. I felt as if they were a revelation even though this information is as old as time. It may be difficult for you to believe this, but I love you dearly, and I consider it a privilege and an honor to be able to share this truth with you. If there is even one thought, idea or tool presented in this book that will help you to improve the quality of your life and add to the joy of your world, it will be worth every electron of energy, time, effort, or money that I have expended in bringing it to you. As you absorb these principles into your being, you will gradually realize that you are merely being reminded of what you already know in your heart.

There are natural laws that govern this universe, and every single person on the planet is subject to them. When we understand these laws and cooperate with them, we can become the masters of our lives. By trying to outsmart or mock these laws, we end up in states of total confusion and despair. Through self-awareness, we can determine how our behavioral patterns, our thoughts, words and actions, our feelings, our worries, our fears and our concerns have created our present life situation. Once we become aware of what it is we are doing that creates the negative circumstances in our lives, we can take very practical, tangible, logical steps to create positive circumstances instead. We are not the victims of circumstance. We have a great deal of control over the things that are taking place in our lives. At any given moment we are a sum total of our behavioral patterns and human responses. Consequently, whether we are talking about our family life, our financial situation, our health, our job, our state of mind or our social life, it matters not. We are responsible for our current state of affairs. This is one of the most difficult natural laws for anyone to accept, but once we accept responsibility for our lives, then we have the power to change them.

When I first became aware of this fundamental truth my reaction was total rebellion. I thought, "Hog-wash! How could I possibly be responsible for the things other people are doing to me?" Fortunately, I had an ever-present drive for knowledge, so I kept studying and searching in every conceivable avenue, and to my amazement, this same concept kept presenting itself to me everywhere I turned. It became clear to me that if I was going to progress I had to get over this hurdle of resistance. Very cautiously I began to think, "What if this really is true? What if I really can turn my life around by controlling my thoughts, words, actions and feelings?" I decided I had nothing to lose by at least accepting this principle as a possibility. Slowly but surely, through trial and error and some very intense personal application, I proved this natural law to my own satisfaction beyond a shadow of a doubt.

This book is based on my findings. I don't ever want you to accept something as truth just because someone has told you it's true. The only way *the truth will set you free* is if you experiment with it, apply it to your life, and prove it to yourself.

2

The Power of Thought

Throughout the history of the world there have been prophets, seers, and philosophers who have proclaimed the coming of an age in which the people of Earth would develop the latent powers within and truly become the creators of their own destiny. World religions have always indicated mankind's responsibility for his or her actions, but for some reason the full import of this message never really registered in our minds. If it had, we would not be in the mess we are in today.

We are now on the threshold of what is being called the New Age, and through the advancement of modern technology, a bridge is being formed between spiritual teachings, philosophy, and scientific discoveries. Even though this science is in its infancy, the basic natural law of action and reaction, like attracts like, or better known as The Law of the Circle, can no longer be written off as religious rhetoric or human conjecture. It is now being proven on a scientific level.

You have probably heard statements such as "As a man thinketh in his heart, so he is," or "The Power of Positive Thinking," or "Thoughts are Things." The truth is that *ENERGY FOLLOWS THOUGHT!* It is being discovered that these statements are not just lofty platitudes, but that thoughts actually involve the law of physics.

In order for us to accept responsibility for our lives and attain self-mastery, it is very important for us to understand the process that occurs through our thoughts, words, actions and feelings, so I'm going to explain this natural Law of the Circle in detail. It may seem a little technical at times, but hang in there. It will be well worth your every effort.

We live, move, breathe, and have our being within an electromagnetic forcefield of energy. The electronic structure of this forcefield has a specific quality and frequency of vibration that is determined by our thoughts, feelings, words, and actions. This electronic energy runs through our body and causes our heart to beat. We cannot take a breath, have a thought, experience a feeling, digest food, or move a muscle without using this energy. Ancient philosophies have been teaching about this energy for thousands of years, but the western world, for the most part, had discounted its existence since science couldn't logically trace the energy fields through the body. Recent research into these supposedly non-existant energy fields has been greatly accelerated. Thanks to modern technology, the scientific world is no longer denying the existence of these forces working through the body.

Soviet scientists have made parapsychology a major thrust in their research for quite some time. In 1968 they announced the discovery of what they felt was a new energy system in human beings. Through Kirlian photography, a high frequency electrical technique, the Soviet scientists were able to photograph energy moving along specific pathways in the body. This is something that the oriental science of acupuncture has been telling humanity for 4,000 years. The Chinese have always called this energy Chi. Until recently western scientists dismissed the science of acupuncture because of their inability to pinpoint these energy pathways. This new method of photography revealed streams of energy moving through the body, sparkling lights, and miniature starbursts. This was considered a major breakthrough in the western world.

Yogis have tried to tell mankind of these energy fields through the science of Yoga for several centuries. They refer to this energy as Prana. Throughout western history this vital energy field in and around the body has been discovered and dismissed and rediscovered time and time again. It has been given numerous names such as vital force, odic force, bio-energy, bioplasma energy, orgon energy, etheric force, bioelectric magnetic energy, and life force. Finally our scientific world agrees that this energy must be dealt with and can no longer be disregarded.

Acupuncture is now being accepted as a science. This science teaches that electrical energy flows through the body on specific meridians, and if this flow of energy is blocked to any of the cells or organs in the body, that part of the body malfunctions and disease sets in. Acupuncture and acupressure unblock the meridians and restore the flow of energy to the affected area. The medical profession is using acupuncture, on occasion, to deliberately block the flow of energy to a specific area of the body to eliminate pain during surgery.

Another new science that is discovering the power of the electrical forcefields is biofeedback. Through biofeedback, electrodes are taped to various points of the body, and through concentration, thought control, deep breathing and relaxation, a person can eliminate stress and pain, slow down the heart rate, reducing the intensity of the flow of blood to the brain, thus getting rid of migraine headaches and assisting in the healing process of the body. The science of Yoga has always practiced these methods, but until the technology was developed to prove it scientifically, people in the western world were generally very skeptical of its effectiveness.

Other things that are being proven through the new forms of technology are that these energy fields are directly affected by a person's emotions, thoughts, health, and state of mind. Kirlian photography has shown that there are definite changes in the radiance, color, shape and intensity of the energy field around a person's body, depending on whether or not he or she is ill or healthy, angry or peaceful, sad or happy.

The polygraph test is another form of technology that has been used in recent times to measure emotional responses. This instrument registers changes in respiration and perspiration that are triggered by electrical impulses in the body. These electrical impulses are affected by our state of mind, our emotions, our fears, and our general well-being.

Tests have been conducted whereby electrodes are taped to a person's head to test the strength of these electromagnetic currents of energy that are sent forth with our thoughts, and in certain states of consciousness, the brain waves have generated enough electricity to move an electric train.

As you know, when someone is critically ill in the hospital, there are various types of monitoring devices now available that continually test the electrical impulses flowing through the heart and brain, and when those electrical impulses cease, when the monitor is flat, we know that the person is no longer in that body. A person cannot even sustain life in the physical realm without using these currents of energy.

Now, what exactly does this information mean in regard to getting our lives in order? This energy field is directly affected by our thoughts, our emotions, our actions, and it is the quality of the vibration of this energy field that determines the things that are taking place in our lives.

This energy comes to us from a source outside of ourselves. We do not generate or create this energy within our being, and when it is withdrawn, we cannot remain in our physical bodies. This energy enters the body through the top of our head in a stream of electrons. People who have a slight degree of etheric vision can see this stream of electrons and have called it a *silver cord*. After the energy enters the top of our head, it descends down the spinal cord through electrical pathways and is distributed throughout the body by means of an electrical system called the Chakras. (The Chakras will be discussed in detail in another chapter.)

When we receive this energy it is pure, neutral and vibrating at a frequency of perfection. This electronic Light substance is truly our life force. You may relate to the *source* of your life force in any way that is comfortable for you. If you relate to it spiritually, you may perceive it as coming forth from the very Heart of God. If you feel more comfortable relating to it philosophically you may identify this source as a Universal Mind. Even if you can relate to this energy source only scientifically as some kind of cosmic generator, for our purpose here, that is perfectly all right, just as long as you understand not one electron comes forth from the Universal Source that is less than perfection.

With every thought we think, every word we speak, every action we take, every emotion we feel, we send this energy forth on an electromagnetic current similar to a radio wave or a television wave. This current of energy goes directly to the person, place, condition, or thing we send it to through our thoughts, actions, words and feelings. This current of energy is vibrating at a particular frequency, and depending on our attitude or our frame of mind at the time we send it forth, that energy could be vibrating at a high constructive frequency of harmony and peace, or it could be vibrating at a heavy discordant frequency of anger or frustration.

We have the free will to accept this gift of life, this pure harmonious energy from the Universal Source, and let it flow through us harmoniously and constructively, or we can intercept this pure energy and misqualify it into discordant vibrations of hatred, anger, frustration, fear, etc. The important thing to understand is that *we are responsible for that decision*.

I would like to share an example of this process with you to make this natural law as graphic and clear as possible. The more you understand this law, the more willing you will be to put forth the effort necessary to transform your life. Let's use love as an example. If someone is sending a thought and feeling of love to another person, it doesn't matter if the person is in the same room or across the globe, that expression of love goes forth on an electromagnetic current of energy straight to the person it is directed to. Love is the cohesive power of the universe, and has one of the highest frequencies of vibration. In science there is an expression of *like attracts like* and as this current of energy passes through the atmosphere to its destination, it draws to itself other energy that is vibrating at the same frequency. In this case we're talking about love, so this current draws to itself other vibrations of love as it travels to its objective. When this energy reaches the person it is directed to, it literally bathes them in the wonderful vibration of love. Nothing is solid; everything is made up of electrons and even smaller particles of energy, so when this love reaches its objective it actually permeates every cell and organ of the person's body, uplifting them and making them feel good, even if they don't understand why, or know that someone is sending them love. It gives them a real blessing. Then, and this is the most important point of all, *that current of energy returns to its point of origin*, the person that sent it forth. On the return current it again draws to itself additional energy vibrating at the same frequency. Consequently, by the time it returns to the sender, it is greatly magnified over what was originally sent out. This is what is known as the Law of the Circle, and remember, it is a natural law that we are all subject to whether we believe in it or not. So, rather than trying to foolishly disprove the natural laws that govern this universe, we need to educate ourselves, learn to cooperate with them; then instead of blundering through lives of chaos and despair, we will consciously create lives of harmony and joy.

When we are talking about vibration, the doctrine of like attracts like is clearly demonstrated and works on the same principle as tuning forks. If you walk into a room filled with tuning forks and strike the note of C on the piano, all of the tuning forks tuned into that frequency begin vibrating and the others do not. If you strike the note of F just the tuning forks tuned to that frequency begin vibrating and the others do not.

In our life the frequency of love attracts love, the frequency of hate attracts hate. Whatever we are sending out through our thoughts, words, actions, and feelings is returning to us greatly magnified. Therefore, what might have seemed like a simple expression of love, by the time it accumulates all the vibrations of love along the way to its destination and again on the return current to us, it could bring enough constructive energy with it to manifest as a real blessing in our life, such as harmonious family relationships, good health, financial prosperity, a fulfilling job, peace of mind, happiness or a multitude of other seemingly unrelated things.

Natural law is accurate to the letter, so if we are sending out the heavy, discordant negative vibrations of hatred, anger, envy, jealousy, resentment, frustration, criticism, fear, depression, anxiety, or even milder negative emotions such as boredom, lethargy or indifference, these currents, too, return to us greatly magnified. What might have seemed like a mild temper tantrum could return with such a momentum of destructive energy that it causes a car accident, an illness, family problems, financial problems, emotional or mental problems, or again, a barrage of other seemingly unrelated things.

This principle will be demonstrated in many different ways throughout this book, so instead of being mind-boggling or mystical, it will be very practical and logical.

There is really no such thing as a neutral thought or feeling. There are positive vibrations and there are negative vibrations. On a percentage basis, if a feeling or thought is 51% or more of a positive frequency or vibration, it means it is more positive than negative, and therefore adds to the overall positive energy on the planet. If a thought or feeling is 51% or more of a negative frequency or vibration, it means it is more negative than positive, and therefore, adds to the overall negative energy on the planet.

I know it is often difficult to accept this principle and acknowledge that we are responsible for our current life situations, but it is a critical factor in gaining control of our lives.

Many people have devastating things happening in their lives, and their actions don't seem to warrant such drastic results. There is an explanation for this.

You must remember that we are talking about every electron of precious life energy we have ever used. We are talking about *every* thought, *every* feeling, *every* word or action. Just for a moment reflect back over your life and think of the literally millions of times that you have had thoughts or feelings that were less than kind or less than harmonious. The majority of people just allow the thoughts of the day to muddle through their minds with very little awareness from the moment they arise in the morning until they go to sleep at night. If you comprehend that every one of those less-than-positive thoughts returns to you greatly magnified over what you sent out, then you may agree it's a wonder you can even stand up under the pressure of that misqualified energy.

Another reason why our life situations sometimes seem out of proportion to our life expressions is because at the present time there is a great deal of negative energy being released on this planet through world governments, poor economy, crime, hatred, war, disease, etc. When we send out these negative thoughts and feelings, there is a tremendous amount of energy vibrating at these negative frequencies to be drawn to our current of energy. For example, if this entire planet were filled with light and love and we had a thought of hate, that current would go out, and with no other hate in the atmosphere, it would return to us with very little ramification. But with the world situation as it is now, when we send forth a thought of hate, there are literally tons of hate that can be drawn to our thought, and the returning current can bombard us with unbelievable amounts of destructive energy.

There is one caution I would like to state at this time. *Never* judge anyone else by what you observe taking place in his or her life. Natural law always returns the *maximum* negative energy to a person that they can withstand at any given time to give them the opportunity to quickly transmute that negativity back into its proper vibration. You *never* know what learning experiences another person is going through. If you observe someone going through an extremely difficult life experience, it may mean that they have released more negative energy than usual, or it may mean they are a very strong and courageous person, and natural law is returning large amounts of their misqualified energy all at once. If you observe someone having a relatively easy-going life, it may mean that they have earned it and released more positive energy than other people, or it may mean that they are a very weak person and can't withstand any more negative energy than that at one time. If the latter is the case, then the weak person will be going through their negative experiences for a much, much longer period of time than the strong, courageous person. The important thing is that you never know what anyone else's life plan is, so please don't judge anyone.

The most constructive thing we can do is to put all of our efforts into learning about ourselves and become the masters of our own lives. Then, through our example, we can help other people learn the process of self-mastery so they can take control of their lives as well.

3

Self-Awareness, The Key to Self-Mastery

Now that we have gotten past some of the technical explanations as to why our lives may be in their present state of disarray, we can begin taking the steps to do something about it.

The first step is to take a good look at ourselves and our lives. In order for us to change our lives into what we really want them to be, we must first be aware of what presently exists. This is a time of evaluation as an *objective observer*. This is not a time to berate, criticize, or condemn ourselves for our past mistakes. That only adds more negative energy to the situation. The purpose of this evaluation is to help us see what it is we like about our lives, and what it is we would like to change. Usually the people I talk to know their lives are not what they should be and may be aware of one major problem, such as finances or health, but they have never actually taken a good look at their overall lives. This is a crucial step toward self-mastery, so invest the time now to take inventory.

Get a piece of paper and write down the various aspects of your life as they exist now. Remember that the purpose of this evaluation is to give you some insight into yourself, so you need to be as honest as you possibly can. Be specific. Some of the areas you may want to look into are: personal relationships involving parents, spouse, children, friends and co-workers; job or career; finances; health, including physical, mental and emotional; social life; spiritual life; attitudes; goals; desires; dreams–to list only a few. Expand on this list and make it as detailed as possible.

Now that you have evaluated your present status, go back over your list and note especially the things you like about your life and the things you would like to improve or change.

In order for you to succeed in transforming your life, you need to see where you are going. You need to have objectives and goals. Most people spend so much time worrying and dwelling on the things that they *don't* want in their lives that they haven't taken the time to figure out what they really *do* want.

What we think about, what we hold in our minds and put our attention and energy into, we actually draw into our lives. So it is time to stop precipitating the things that we don't want and start drawing to ourselves the things that we do want.

Everything that exists on the planet at the present time exists because someone is holding it in their consciousness. For example, if at this very moment, no one ever again thought of war, that entity would be dissipated. Governments would not be raising budgets to create a greater war machine, the military would not be training for battle, people would stop inventing and building weapons, and countries would stop planning the invasion of other countries. That may seem a little hard to believe, but think about it for a minute. If war was not part of our consciousness, it would not be part of our human behavior.

As you begin learning more and more about yourself through observation, you will be amazed at how often you allow negative thoughts and feelings to be the focal point of your attention. The age-old admonition *Man know thyself* is the key to self-mastery. Patterns of thinking and emotional responses are usually habits we have allowed ourselves to develop without much conscious awareness at all. Now that you have decided to take charge of your life, you no longer need to just muddle through the day. Instead, you can deliberately control your thoughts, words, actions and feelings. Since it is a natural law that what you put your attention and energy into, you draw into your life, it is only logical that you take the steps necessary to let go of destructive programming and begin creating for yourself a fulfilling, happy, harmonious, peaceful life.

People, when asked, rarely feel they are negative; so, one of the things I have them do is keep a scratch tally for an entire week of every negative thought or feeling they experience. Notice I said *every* negative thought or feeling. This includes the little, trivial, petty things that you allow to pop into your mind, such as the person that pulled in front of your car that you thought was a jerk, or the service you received that you felt was lousy, or the lady at the supermarket that you thought was ugly, or the disgust you had for yourself for overeating, or the anger you felt because the car broke down, and so on.

My experience has been that even so-called positive people return with several sheets of tally marks and are astounded at how often they were negative and shocked at how oblivious they were about their negative thinking. So, the next step toward your self-mastery is to observe your daily responses for an entire week, pay very close attention to your thoughts and feelings and keep a scratch tally of every negative thought or feeling you have.

This is a very valuable exercise because it clearly shows how many times every single day you are misqualifying energy without even realizing it.

Many of the people I have worked with have fallen into the *poor me* syndrome. They feel that they are really *good* people, but all of these terrible things keep happening to them anyway. What this exercise reveals is that we may not be doing catastrophic negative things like mugging people or robbing a bank, but we are often nickel-and-diming ourselves to death with trivial pettiness.

Once you complete this exercise and acknowledge that you may not be controlling your thoughts or feelings, but just allowing them to happen, you can move on to the next step of changing those bad habits and begin to take control of your thoughts, words and deeds.

There has been a lot of research done on the process of changing a habit, and the general concensus is that it takes twenty-one consecutive days to change a habit. We are talking about a lifetime of unmonitored, uncontrolled thinking; it is not practical to expect total self-mastery overnight. You must be consistent and patient with yourself. I am going to give you some exercises that will help you become more and more aware of your thoughts and feelings.

Each time you put forth the effort to deliberately program yourself into constructive thinking, the stronger you will become and the more natural the positive response will be. Before you know it, your pattern of thinking will automatically be positive instead of negative, and you will have established a new constructive habit.

While you are going through this process of gaining control of your thoughts and feelings, you need to be tolerant and forgiving of yourself. If you find negative thinking or negative feelings creeping into your consciousness, you need to stop, empty your mind of the negative thought or feeling, take a deep breath, regroup, and then look for the positive side of the situation you are dealing with. Don't give any more power to the negative thought by berating or condemning yourself for the transgression. Just let it go, and magnify the positive side of the situation, no matter how small.

The first exercise to begin your new habit of positive thinking is to look for the positive side of every person, place, condition or thing you encounter. The general rule is that we can easily spot the flaws in other people, but unless someone is a genius or looks like a Greek God, we rarely notice their positive attributes. In this exercise you must go out of your way to search for something good in every single thing you come in contact with. Sometimes this is a real challenge. Some people you know may seem so objectionable that the only thing you will be able to appreciate about them is the color of their socks, but you *must* find something good in every instance.

After practicing this for a while, you will come to the realization that, no matter how bad things seem or how degenerate a person may appear, there is a spark of hope in every situation and a spark of light in every person. By consciously putting your attention on that one redeeming quality, rather than giving momentum and power to the negative, you can turn that destructive situation into a positive experience, and you can often give the negative person the incentive he or she needs to find a better way of behaving. This may sound too good to be true, but I assure you this natural law is as accurate and workable as the laws of mathematics, music, physics, or any other science.

The next exercise I have found to be very helpful in assisting people to learn more about their behavioral responses is to have each one keep a daily chart of their overall feelings. I call this chart a *Mood Sheet*. We have cycles in which we are more *up* mentally, physically, and emotionally, and cycles in which we are more *down*. The purpose of the *Mood Sheet* is for each person to become more aware of his or her own individual cycles, so that he or she can work with them instead of just obliviously blundering along.

On the left hand side of the *Mood Sheet* are listed various states of emotions that we might experience daily from the lowest to the highest. These emotions are given a certain number value, with a plus for positive emotions and a minus for negative emotions. Across the top of the chart are listed the days of the month. At the end of each day, evaluate what your *predominant* emotion was for the day and put a dot on the chart under the day of the month next to the corresponding emotion. (See Figure 1, Page 21.) You can then draw a line connecting the dots and you will have a graph showing specific cycles of up and down periods. The advantage of knowing about these cycles is that when you know you are coming into a down period, you can exert a little more effort and pull yourself up instead of just allowing yourself to slip into negative patterns.

The *Mood Sheet* is very easy to do and it takes very little time, but it keeps you conscious of your emotions and helps you to gain control of them. I recommend that you keep this graph continually throughout your learning process.

Something that completely amazes me is that I have often heard people say they can't imagine anything more boring than living in harmony all of the time. They feel that without the low lows they can't experience the high highs. What I have observed in these people is that they are not experiencing the high highs at all, but merely vacillating from the low lows to what we call neutral. There are so many octaves of wonderful emotions above harmony they have not even glimpsed yet because they are struggling so hard just to keep their heads above water. The more we become masters of our lives, the more we will be able to experience the higher and higher octaves of perfection. For example, above harmony are beautiful feelings of bliss, ecstasy, elation, wonder, awe, and innumerable feelings we don't even have words to describe. I promise you there will be nothing boring about living a life of pure uninterrupted harmony.

The next exercise is designed to help you reprogram your thinking with positive affirmations. People who have used positive affirmations have always known they work, but rarely understood exactly why. Now, with more and more research, we are learning how the process works. Through positive affirmations, we can deliberately send forth constructive thoughtforms that will accumulate additional positive energy

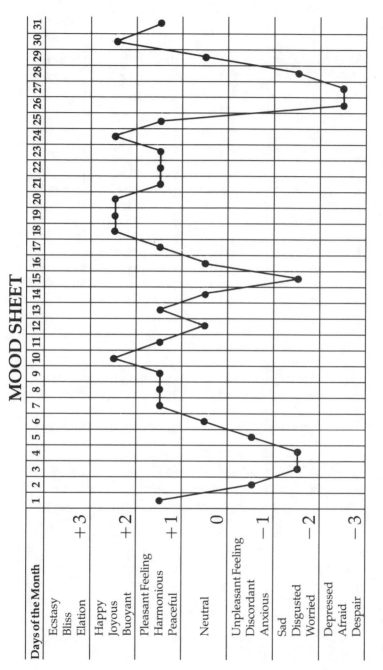

FIGURE 1

MOOD SHEET

Days of the Month	1	2	3	4	5	6	7	8	9	10	11	12	13	14	15	16	17	18	19	20	21	22	23	24	25	26	27	28	29	30	31
Ecstasy / Bliss / Elation +3																															
Happy / Joyous / Buoyant +2																															
Pleasant Feeling / Harmonious / Peaceful +1																															
Neutral 0																															
Unpleasant Feeling / Discordant / Anxious −1																															
Sad / Disgusted / Worried −2																															
Depressed / Afraid / Despair −3																															

FIGURE 1A

and return to us, bringing to us what we are affirming.

The difference between a prayer and an affirmation is that in prayer we are usually humbly asking for something, and in an affirmation we are actually commanding Universal Light substance to flow through us constructively to create whatever perfection it is we are affirming.

There is another very important reason why affirmations work, and I would like to share it with you. I am not teaching *religion* in this book, and I have no intention of infringing on anyone's spiritual beliefs, but this point is another aspect of natural law. When we make a positive affirmation we generally begin with the words "I Am". These two words serve as a code word that tunes us into the Universal Source of All Life. Throughout the history of science we have studied this universe, and whether we are studying the most minute particle of life through a microscope, or the farthest reaches of the universe through a powerful telescope, the only thing we have discovered exists is energy. Everything is comprised of this electronic light substance vibrating at different frequencies with various densities. The words "I Am" reflect this all-encompassing Oneness of all Life. "I" represents Alpha or the beginning, "Am" represents Omega or the ending, meaning this Unversal Source of All Life is the beginning and the ending of all that exists. In eastern philosophies, the word "Om" has been used as a chant or a mantra to raise the consciousness of the devotee. "Om" is the Sanskrit word for "I Am." In the Bible, when Moses spoke to the burning bush and said "Who are you?", the reply was "I Am That I Am." "I Am Alpha, I Am Omega."

When we *invoke* this Universal Light Substance to flow through us with our affirmations or our thoughts, words, actions or feelings, it automatically obeys. A very important thing to realize is that when we use the code words "I Am," it is actually an invocation. It is part of the natural law of the universe that anything we state following this invocation *has to manifest*.

Once this information registers in our consciousness, then we will understand that by making negative statements about ourselves, we are actually invoking the very situation we are bemoaning. We will understand how foolish it is to say things such as "I Am" sick, "I Am" tired, "I Am" angry, "I Am" poor, "I Am" lonely, etc. Each time such statements are made the electronic energy *must* flow through us with the frequency of vibration we have just invoked.

Fortunately, a positive affirmation is also an invocation and a command for this Universal Light Substance to manifest as something good in our lives.

The following affirmations are designed to help us begin re-programming our negative thinking into positive thinking. The longer that energy is accustomed to flowing through the brain in a particular pattern, the easier it is to just keep flowing in the same pattern. For instance, if we are used to being critical or judgmental of others, that is a pattern we have developed and the energy flows very easily into that "groove" of the brain. If we want to change that habit, we have to consciously begin developing a new "groove" through which this energy can flow. The more we withhold the energy from the negative, critical pattern and send it forth through the new constructive pattern, the sooner we will have changed the bad habit.

It might help to visualize this as a river. The more the water flows through the river, the deeper and wider the river becomes and the easier the water flows. But, if we create a new channel and divert the water, gradually the old river will dry up and cease to be, and the new channel will eventually become as deep and wide as the previous river.

I would like to give you a word of encouragement at this point. I know when we first begin observing our behavioral responses, we are usually shocked and a little overwhelmed at how ingrained our trivial, petty patterns are, and it seems as though it will be a monumental task to overcome them. However, once you begin to consciously take control of these patterns, changes will take place much more quickly than you can envision. Before you know it, the positive patterns will be deeply ingrained and the negative patterns won't even be a part of your consciousness anymore. This is true with any new lesson you are learning. Once you have mastered the lesson, it's a "piece of cake."

As an example, it probably wouldn't even enter your mind to mug someone, or rob a bank, or kill someone because somewhere along the line you have already learned the lesson that that is not suitable behavior. These aren't feelings that you have to struggle with every day or continually monitor or try to change. They're simply not part of your consciousness. I assure you, once you really develop the habit of positive thinking, the critical, petty, trivial things that so easily pop into your mind now won't even be part of your consciousness.

With positive affirmations, we are beginning to form the new constructive "grooves" in our thinking patterns. For this reason it is important to read the affirmations the first thing in the morning and the last thing before going to bed at night. The exercise in the morning will begin the constructive flow of energy through the brain and set your attitude for the entire day.

The exercise at night will help by drawing the principles of the positive affirmations into your subconscious mind; so, you can reprogram yourself while you sleep, as in sleep learning. Research is proving that what we think about at night before we go to sleep is carried into the subconscious mind, so it is a good idea to put your attention on something constructive. For heaven's sake, don't watch the news just before going to sleep!

Strive to consciously apply the principles in the affirmations throughout your daily activities.

Beginning Today...

1. *I AM in such control of my emotions that nothing can disturb my peace of mind.*

2. *I AM WATCHING my words, thoughts and actions because they are all-powerful and will bring their effect into my life. I can rule my world and all outer conditions.*

3. *I AM letting my family and friends know that they are a vital, significant part of my life and I AM as enthusiastic about their accomplishments as I am about my own accomplishments.*

4. *I AM speaking of Health, Happiness, and Prosperity to every person I meet and magnifying the positive side of every situation no matter how small.*

5. *I AM so involved with improving myself that I do not have time to notice or criticize the shortcomings of others.*

6. *I AM giving thanks for every circumstance in every move of my life. For in true heartlifting thanks I can reach that faith which removes mountains.*

7. *I AM quieting myself for a few minutes each morning, emptying my mind of all thoughts and LISTENING for the voice of my higher-self for guidance and illumination.*

8. *I AM a radiating center of Love, Peace, Happiness and Harmony.*

9. *I AM thinking only of the best, speaking only of the best, doing only the best, and* EXPECTING *only the best.*

10. *I AM giving a smile to every living creature I meet today for I know every impulse for a thoughtful act, every single smile given from a heart filled with love, every kind word spoken, when a hasty word would have been so much easier, is a small gift of love I AM able to return for the many blessings I have received.*

11. *I AM engulfing every electron of precious life energy evolving on this Sweet Earth with the essence of pure love.*

Summary of the Beginning Steps
to Self-Awareness

1. As an objective observer evaluate your life and write down the various aspects as they exist now. Areas to look into are:

>   Personal Relationships
>   Career or Job
>   Finances
>   Health
>   Social Life
>   Spiritual Life
>   Attitudes
>   Goals
>   Desires
>   Dreams

2. Go over your evaluation and note what you like about your life and what you would like to change or improve.

3. For one week continually monitor your thoughts and keep a simple scratch tally of every negative thought or feeling that pops into your mind.

4. Consciously look for the positive side of every person, place, condition, or thing you come in contact with. Then accentuate that positive quality or aspect, no matter how small it seems to be.

5. Monitor your feelings throughout the day and at the end of each day note on the Mood Sheet your predominant feeling.

6. Begin reprogramming your thinking process by stating the positive affirmations of the *Beginning Today*...sheet first thing in the morning and in the evening before you retire. Then strive to apply the principles of the affirmations throughout the day.

4

Attaining Goals Through Creative Visualization

Since we draw into our lives whatever it is we put our attention and energy into, it is only logical and practical for us to put our attention and energy into the things we want, rather than the things we don't want.

Children have a wonderful sense of imagination. They can sit for hours daydreaming and pretending they are all sorts of marvelous things. Unfortunately, as they get older, they are told by supposedly knowledgable and well-meaning adults that they are wasting their time, and that it is not practical to daydream or imagine they're something they're not. Thus, this creative ability is stifled and pushed back into an obscure corner of their minds. You can probably remember such instances in your own life.

We are learning more and more about the mysteries of this incredible instrument, the human mind. We have discovered that the physical brain structure is divided into two separate hemispheres. For a long time we have known that the left hemisphere of the brain is the portion that contains the rational, logical mind, but until recently, scientists believed that the right hemisphere was dormant. With new research, we are now discovering that the right hemisphere is not only not dormant, but it is our creative center, and contains our ability to imagine and visualize. We are discovering that by consciously using both hemispheres of the brain in a cooperative effort, we can create anything in our lives we can imagine.

This may seem a little difficult for some to believe, but there are some very real changes that occur in our mind, body and environment when we deliberately apply the laws of creative visualization.

First, let's look deeper into the activities of the two hemispheres of the brain. The general learning activities of the left hemisphere of the brain tend to be:

> Intellectual
> Rational
> Logical
> Linear
> Sequential
> Focused
> Discriminative
> Verbal (Words and sentences)
> Deductive
> Explicit
> Active
> Analytical
> Goal-centered

With the above learning activities of the left brain, the learning preferences tend to be:

> Defining
> Clarifying (Separating)
> Organizing Information
> Questioning
> Verifying
> Planning
> Writing
> Talking

The learning activites of the right hemisphere of the brain tend to be quite different. They are:

> Emotional
> Nonrational (Fantasy, curiosity)
> Intuitive
> Nonlinear
> Simultaneous
> Diffused
> Integrative
> Timeless
> Imaginative
> Visualization (Images)
> Experiential
> Receptive
> Experience-centered

The learning preferences of the right brain tend to be:

> Wondering
> Creating
> Dreaming
> Drawing
> Singing
> Feelings
> Visualizing
> Unifying
> Combining in unusual ways
> Imagining

By merging the dual activities of the rational, logical mind with the imaginative, creative mind, we open ourselves up to the creative flow of this universe that will enable us to become the masters of our lives rather than the victims of our lives.

The process that takes place when we put our attention and energy into something and draw it into our lives is the same whether we do this consciously and deliberately or whether we do this unconsciously by accident, because the law is the law, no matter how it is applied.

At this point on our path to self-mastery, we have learned

why the negative circumstances are taking place in our lives. We have evaluated how we have misqualified energy with our thoughts, feelings, words, and actions. We have decided what we like and don't like about our lives, and we have begun to take the steps to retrain ourselves to think constructively rather than negatively. It is time now to begin creating what we really want in our lives. It is time to set our goals and use the tools available to us to draw into our lives our hopes, dreams, and desires. We need to reach back into that obscure corner of our minds where we shoved our gift of imagination and bring it out, polish it up and put it to work.

The first step is to set our goal. We need to decide on something we would like to work toward, have, realize, or create. In determining our goals, we must bear in mind the following principles. This goal must be constructive, honorable and worthy of our time and effort. It must be honest, both to ourselves and to the rest of the world. It should not be just for a whim or for gratifying the appetites of the physical senses. We need to be sure there are no lurking feelings that we would be glad to benefit at the expense of anyone else. There is no mocking natural law, and anything contrary to this will draw an even greater momentum of negative energy and destruction into our lives. This goal can be on any level. It can be a change in ourselves, a relationship, a job, increased financial freedom, a happier state of mind, improved health, a home, beauty, better physical condition, or whatever we can imagine.

It is a good idea to choose goals that are fairly easy to believe in at the beginning, goals that you will be able to reach in the fairly near future. That way, as you are learning this process of creative visualization, you can maximize your feelings of success and lower the negative resistance in yourself. When you have more practice you will be able to take on more difficult and challenging problems.

I have been asked whether or not there is such a thing as an unrealistic goal. I know there is a great deal of controversy over statements such as *You can be whatever you want to be*, but, I truly believe you *can* be whatever you *want* to be with, of course, certain exceptions. Obviously a man cannot have a baby, or a woman cannot be the King of England. However, each of us has a super-conscious mind that operates only in the realms of perfection. This super intelligence is continually prodding and prompting us on to reach our highest potential. This *higher self* is absolutely aware of our gifts, talents, abilities, and our reason for being in the physical plane, and it perpetually guides, directs and prompts us toward the fulfillment of our life purpose. These promptings come to our conscious mind in the form of a heart call, or our wants and desires. If we will quiet ourselves and listen for the "still, small voice" of our higher self we will *want* to be only that which we have the ability to attain.

After we have chosen a goal, the next step is to get a clear mental picture or idea of the goal. We must visualize the goal already completed or accomplished exactly as we want it to be. We need to continually operate in the present tense, the eternal moment of NOW, accepting that our goal already exists in every detail in our consciousness, and the more attention and energy we put into it, the more quickly it will be brought into a physical manifestation. Now that we know more about the mechanics of thought, we know that a thought is actually the link between the unformed world and the physical realm. Thought is the blueprint that begins bringing our goal into a tangible reality. After we have a crystal-clear mental picture of our goal in every detail, we should write it down on paper. This act brings our goal from the realm of consciousness into the realm of form. This is the first impulse of our goal from the fourth-dimensional world into the third-dimensional world.

After this is accomplished, we need to focus on our goal often. Read it over often and frequently bring it to mind through mental pictures. This should be done in quiet periods of meditation, as well as casually throughout the day as we go about our daily activities. The more we familiarize ourselves with our goal, the more it will become an integrated part of our life. It will become more real, and we can project it more successfully. Focus on it clearly and yet in a light, gentle way. The more details we have, the better. If we set an abstract, ephemeral goal such as *I want happiness* then our blueprint is hazy and confused. What is happiness? If you want happiness, then evaluate in great detail what happiness means to you. If it means prosperity, harmonious relationships, good health, a fulfilling job, etc., then include the details of all of these concepts in your goal.

When we are working with mental pictures, it is important to know that visualization is a very individual thing. Some of the people I work with, when asked to visualize something, see a three-dimensional moving picture as if they were just watching a movie. Others don't *see* anything, but rather have a feeling or an impression of the object they are asked to visualize. The important point is that however you visualize is perfectly all right and works just as effectively as any other method of visualization.

To find out just how you visualize, take a moment and close your eyes, then draw to your mind the mental picture of the face of a dear friend. However that friend appears is how you personally visualize. Some people will see a crystal clear image as though the friend were standing before them, others will see a vague image, others will just have an impression or a feeling about the friend, and still others will only remember the friend. Any of these methods is just fine. Many times people become frustrated and give up trying to reach their goal because they say they can't visualize. Everyone can visualize. It is just the form that is different.

When you are focusing on your goal during the day, both during periods of meditation and casually as you go about your daily activities, deliberately give it positive energy. The majority of our energy is released through our feelings and our emotions, so the more we can experience the success of accomplishing our goal in our feeling worlds, the more quickly it will be realized. As we visualize our goal already completed, we should feel the buoyancy and joy of that success, continually thinking of our goal in a positive, encouraging way. The energy that we expend in thinking about our goal must always be light and joyful. If we start becoming uptight about it or expressing any tension during our periods of visualization, we will actually be hindering, rather than helping, the situation.

Positive affirmations are a very effective way of giving added positive energy to our goal. At the end of this chapter I will list several affirmations to give you an idea of the many things you can affirm, but the sky is the limit, and it is better to create your own affirmations tailored to your specific goal.

During the process of creative visualization there are some cautionary points we must be aware of. I call these points "The Imperatives." First, there is the admonition *Tell no man*. It is imperative that you do not discuss your goal with anyone. The reason for this is that you are working with a very delicate process. When you have decided on a goal through the process of thought, you have actually projected a thoughtform or blueprint into the ethers of the electromagnetic forcefield that surrounds you. Remember: *thoughts are things.* As you deliberate on your goal and give it positive energy, you are drawing the Universal Light Substance into your thoughtform and creating a magnet that will draw your goal into the physical realm. If you have discussed your plan with someone else, no matter how loving and supportive they may be, they might have underlying feelings that you are not going to be able to attain your goal. Even if they don't verbally express these doubts, they are sending destructive energy into your thoughtform and dissipating your efforts. In addition to those who lovingly support you, there are those who don't understand, and therefore, feel threatened or jealous, and they will intentionally send negative energy into your thoughtform. So the best general rule is not to discuss your goal with anyone.

The next imperative is for you not to doubt or fear. If you begin to doubt your ability to accomplish your goal or fear that you will somehow fail, then you are sending the same destructive lightning bolts into your thoughtform that you are trying to prevent other people from sending.

The next imperative is not to mix negative thoughts or feelings with your plan. You must *never* be willing to attain your goal at the expense of anyone else. Carefully monitor your feelings, and if your motives are not honorable, or if you are experiencing feelings of greed, selfishness, indifference to others or any other unacceptable emotion, you need to re-evaluate your goal. It is very easy to broaden your goal to include the best for all people concerned. For instance, if your goal is to receive a promotion in your job, but there is already someone employed in the position you are seeking, you should include as part of your goal the thought that that person will move into a more rewarding, fulfilling position as well. Never wish for someone to get fired or removed in any negative way, just so you can attain your goal. Always look at the entire picture and include the best for all concerned.

The next imperative is not to acknowledge a condition less than perfection. We do this when we really don't believe we can have the best or deserve the best. The principles of natural law are just as accurate, whether we are holding a thoughtform of perfection or a thoughtform of destruction. So, go for it! If you are suffering from a physical illness and in a great deal of pain, don't set a goal to just get rid of the pain. Eliminating the pain would be wonderful, but it doesn't do anything to heal your physical body, so eliminate the pain and visualize perfect health at the same time. Don't just eliminate fighting in a relationship, but create real joy and happiness, too.

The next imperative is not to have a set time for your goal to manifest. I know this contradicts many theories on setting goals, but there is a very good reason for this. Natural law is scientific and works accurately to the letter. As soon as we have thought of our goal, we have projected our blueprint into the ethers, so on the fourth-dimensional plane our goal is manifested instantly. The length of time it then takes to be magnetized into the physical plane is determined by our ability to project constructive energy into the thoughtform. That is why we must not arbitrarily set a time limit, but rather work in the eternal moment of NOW, as though our goal were already complete in every detail. We need to know, accept, feel and experience that our goal is accomplished. It is this feeling of the buoyancy of success that will give us the momentum to draw our goals into our lives much more quickly.

When we set a time limit, we actually interfere with the process of natural law. For instance, if we set a goal for six months and program that into our thoughtform, and it would actually be possible for us to accomplish our goal in two months, in all probability we would delay that success and not reach our goal for six months. If we set a goal of six months and our goal was actually going to take two years, at the end of six months we would feel like we had failed and probably give up. Then our goal would never be realized.

So, work in the eternal moment of NOW, accepting that your goal is accomplished and perfect in every detail at this very moment and continue holding the thoughtform of perfection. Then as quickly as you have magnetized enough energy from the Universal Source into your goal, it will be drawn into a physical manifestation.

As you are applying these steps of creative visualization and striving toward your goal, you should continually monitor your feelings and work with this process until you achieve your goal or no longer desire to do so. It is important to know that as we grow and progress toward self-mastery, our goals often grow with us. Many times they will be changed or modified as we go along, which is a perfectly natural part of the human process of change and growth. Don't try to prolong a goal any longer than you have energy for it. If you lose interest in it, it's time to take a new look at what you want. If you find that a goal has changed, acknowledge that fact and get it clear in your mind that you are ending the cycle on the old goal and beginning a new one. This will help to avoid feeling like you've failed when you have simply changed your goal. It's also important to acknowledge when you have reached your goal. Enjoy that feeling of accomplishment and success and thank the universe for fulfilling your request.

Our ability to draw this Universal Light Substance and create perfection in our life is part of our learning experience here on Earth. If we will think about it for a minute, we will realize that the major things we don't like about our lives are being sustained in our lives by following these same steps for creative visualization. Let's take financial problems, for instance. We think about them, which creates the blueprint. We focus on them often by worrying constantly. We have a clear mental picture of all of the things we don't want, such as foreclosure on the house or car, creditors calling, gas and electric being shut off, no money to buy food or clothing, bills piling up, and on and on. We even make negative affirmations continually by stating "I am broke," "I don't have any money," "I can't afford it," "I am unable to pay," "I am having financial problems," etc.

I want to state again that our learning experience in the physical plane is to learn how to work with natural law effectively and become the masters of energy, and ultimately, our lives, rather than the victims of our own misqualified energy. We can do this in one of two ways. We can put forth the effort to educate ourselves, learn the process of how we are affected by this energy and cooperate with it, or we can learn through the *school of hard knocks*, which is trial and error. Either way the result is the same, that *eventually* we will learn how self-defeating it is to misqualify energy, and how by cooperating with natural law, we can create fulfilling, harmonious lives.

In studying world religions, I have come to appreciate that

despite the obvious differences, if we will quiet ourselves and listen to what each other is saying, we will realize we are all saying the same thing in relationship to our responsibility as members of the human race. The bottom line of every world religion is that we have the responsibility to be the best we can be. We have an *obligation* for our gift of life, to reach our highest potential and add to the constructive energy on this Earth. By putting forth the effort to do this, we will discover we can truly turn our lives around and create for ourselves a haven of harmony and peace.

Throughout history we have heard philosphers talk of a day when humanity would experience "Heaven on Earth." This perfection is already pulsating in the ethers at this very moment. We have the opportunity and the ability to magnetize it into our lives. What are we waiting for?

Summary of the Process
of Creative Visualization

Seven Steps:
1. Set Your Goal.
2. Conceive your goal clearly in your mind in every detail.
3. Write your goal down on paper.
4. Visualize your goal already completed.
5. Focus on it often.
6. Give it Positive Energy.
7. Feel the buoyancy of accomplishment and SUCCESS.

Imperatives:
1. Do not discuss your goal with anyone.
2. Do not doubt or fear.
3. Do not mix negative thoughts or feelings with your plan.
4. Do not acknowledge a condition less than perfection.
5. Do not have a set time for your goal to manifest.

Things to Keep in Mind:
1. Your ability to draw perfection into your life is part of your natural learning experience on Earth.
2. When you create something it is actually the Universal Source of all Life acting within you.
3. It is the power of this Universal Light that is accomplishing the goal.
4. The greater the intensity of your visualization and feeling, the more quickly your goal will be drawn into the physical realm.
5. When you use all of the constructive processes it is impossible to fail because it is in agreement with natural law.
6. You are part of the Natural Law of this Universe.
7. Perfection can manifest instantly with the first constructive thoughtform.
8. Every electron of constructive energy belonging to, or serving the Earth at this time has absolute faith in your

ability to succeed.

Remember... "I hold a doctrine, to which I owe not much, but all the little I ever had, namely, that with ordinary talent and extraordinary perserverance, *all* things are attainable."

T.F. Buxton

Positive Affirmations

1. I Am the master of my Life.
2. I Am a radiant person filled with peace and harmony.
3. I Am whole and complete in myself.
4. I Love and appreciate myself as I Am.
5. I Am getting better and better everyday in every way.
6. I Am continually projecting forth Light and Love.
7. I Am an open channel for the creative energy of this Universe.
8. I Am open to receive all of the blessings this abundant Universe has to offer.
9. I Am enjoying putting forth the effort to draw perfection into my Life.
10. I Am now attuned to the perfect plan of my Life.
11. I Am now able to recognize, accept and follow this perfect plan of my Life as it is revealed to me step by step.
12. I Am cognizant that all things are working together for good in my Life.
13. I Am experiencing the pure electronic light substance from the Universal Source of all Life, producing perfect results in every phase of my Life now.
14. Regarding my relationships, I Am...
    Attracting happy, loving, fulfilling relationships into my Life now.
    I love to love and be loved.
    My love is continually expanding and the more I love myself, the more love I have to give others.
    I Am now able to give and receive love freely.
    I Am able to communicate effectively with everyone I come in contact with.

I Am a Peace Commanding Presence wherever I Am.

I Am an example to inspire others to reach their highest potential.

I Am a source of comfort and love for those in despair.

I Am a source of strength and support for every man, woman and child within my sphere of influence.

15. Regarding my Prosperity, I Am...

Thoroughly enjoying my satisfying, well-paying job.

I Am richly rewarded, both creatively and financially.

I Am a source of encouragement and love to my fellow co-workers.

I Am able to ease the burden of others through joy and happiness.

I know that abundance is my natural state of being, and I accept it now.

The supply of the Universe is limitless, and there is plenty for all of us.

Infinite riches are freely flowing into my Life.

I Am growing more financially prosperous each day.

The more I have, the more I have to share.

The more I share, the more I receive and the more fulfilled I feel.

I can be of far greater service and help many more people if I have money than I can if I don't, and as of this moment I choose prosperity.

16. Regarding my health, I Am...

Vibrantly healthy and radiantly beautiful.

I Am a clear channel for the currents of healing energy into the physical realm.

I Am able to restore my mind and body into expressions of perfect health.

The Light within me is creating miracles in my Life here and now.

I accept, in deep humility and gratitude, my Life of health, wealth, happiness and perfect self-expression.

17.   Regarding my state of mind, I Am...
      Experiencing the buoyant joy of self-mastery.
      My life is unfolding in total perfection.
      I Am having fun and enjoying my life.
      I Am relaxed and at peace with myself and the rest of the
      world.
      From my new higher consciousness I Am able to ap-
      preciate the Oneness of All Life.
      I Am able to greet each particle of life with respect and
      reverence.
      I Am happy and blissful just being alive.
      I Am Love!
      I Am Harmony!
      I Am Peace!
      I Am Light!

5

Transforming Your Relationships Through the Power of Unconditional Love

Through the application of unconditional love, it is possible to transform your relationships with your family members, friends, neighbors, co-workers and associates from sources of tension, anxiety, frustration, and often even anger and hatred, into avenues of love, harmony, comfort, joy, and even peace and serenity. This chapter is designed to help you, through self-awareness, learn to use your love and energy as a positive force in your life.

Love is something we've heard the poets and songwriters expound on since the beginning of time, and yet it is still a very misunderstood, and often elusive, concept.

First of all, we must explore the scientific laws that govern love. Love is the most powerful force in the universe. It is not the sentimental, impractical, surface affection that most people have given it credit for. It is literally the cohesive power of the universe, and it is the frequency of the vibration of love that creates the gravitational pull that holds the elements of the Earth together and holds the planets, the stars, and the suns of this universe in their proper orbits.

Love embraces within its sphere of radiation all of the other positive qualities of life. It embraces faith, kindness, hope, patience, charity, forgiveness, mercy, compassion, unselfishness, courage, peace, contentment, happiness, joy, beauty, well-being, opulence, and friendship, to name just a few.

Love is a scientific law. It is a principle. In our own individual life, love is a decision, a consciously maintained attitude of radiation or expression. The aura of love is Light, and if we draw this force into our lives and consciously surround ourselves with this vibration, we can be a peace commanding presence, no matter where we are.

In the first chapters of this book, we learned that, at any given moment, our life situation is a sum total of our thoughts, words, and deeds. We learned that the electronic energy we are continually using to think, move, feel, breathe, and live in in the physical realm is a gift of life that is given to us in a pure and neutral state. As we send this energy forth into the atmosphere with our thoughts, words, actions, and feelings, we have the free will to let it pass through us harmoniously and constructively or to intercept that pure energy and misqualify it into discord and inharmony. What we must always keep in mind is that *we are responsible for that decision.*

This electronic energy is intelligent life. It has a degree of consciousness, and its purpose is to serve life. To help us get a clearer picture of this fact, all we have to do is observe our physical bodies. The cells and organs of our bodies are composed of this exact same electronic energy. Each cell is a miniature universe of orbiting atoms, electrons, neutrons, protons, and even smaller particles of energy that science hasn't identified yet. These cells have an intelligence of their own, apart and separate from our conscious minds. We eat food, and our bodies convert it into various cells. These can be heart cells, blood cells, kidney cells, stomach cells, skin cells, hair cells, liver cells, nail cells, etc. Each of these cells has a very different function and service to perform, and they know just what to do without any conscious direction from us at all. Our bodies are intelligent organisms, and the electronic energy we continually use is intelligent as well.

It is important to register in our minds the fact that we are dealing with intelligent life. Once we accept this truth, it will help us to be more responsible about how we use or abuse this energy. What actually takes place is that this electronic substance comes forth from the Universal Source of all Life vibrating at the octaves of perfection. It is joyous, buoyant energy, eagerly entering its service to life. Either we receive this life energy and allow it to pass through us in harmony, which is a blessing, or else we intercept it and send it forth as a discordant mutation that causes friction and adds to the chaos on this planet.

Once the energy has passed through us into the physical realm, it will remain as part of the overall energy of the Earth. There is no way of destroying energy. All we can do is to transmute the negative energy back into its original vibration by sending positive energy into it. Consequently, the mutations we have sent forth will keep returning to us over and over again until we transmute them back into the frequency of harmony. As we discussed previously, each time this energy returns, it is greatly magnified over what we originally sent out because of the energy of a like nature that it accumulates along the way.

This energy returns through the normal avenues of our lives. Natural law uses whatever means are available to bring this energy back to give us the opportunity to transmute it into its proper vibration. For instance, it can be brought to us through our interpersonal relationships, our jobs, our health, or whatever other vehicles are available.

Once we realize and accept that every experience and expression in our lives is natural law, *in kindness*, returning the energy which we have sent forth, either to bless us if the energy was constructive, or to give us the opportunity to transmute it back to perfection if it was a distorted mutation of destructive energy, then we will be able to look at our trials and tribulations as opportunities rather than with resentment and rebellion.

Regardless of the means natural law uses to return our mis-qualified energy, whether it is through family problems, problems with other relationships, problems with work, finances, health, or whatever, *THERE IS NO INDIVIDUAL PERSON, PLACE, CONDITION, OR THING WHICH CAN RETURN OR INJECT ANYTHING INTO OUR PERSONAL EXPERIENCES WHICH WE HAVE· NOT, IN THE FIRST INSTANCE, CREATED.*

I know that is an awesome statement, but it is from the realm of Illumined Truth. We have all heard the maxim "The truth will set you free," but it is only if we accept the truth, apply it to our lives, and make it part of our lives' expression, that we experience freedom.

Every single person on this planet is special and unique. There are no two people alike, as is evidenced by our finger-prints. Something that has not actually been proven on a scientific level, but that ancient philosophy has been teaching for thousands of years, is that as this electronic energy passes through our heart's center into the world of form, it is stamped with our own individual electronic pattern. I believe, with our new technology, it is going to be just a matter of time until this can be proven. This explains how natural law can determine what energy belongs to whom, and with our own electronic pattern stamped on it, there is no way we can disclaim ownership of the returning negative energy.

Every time I give a lecture and share this information, the question always arises, "What about children? How could a newborn baby that is deformed or retarded be responsible for its circumstances?" This is a very delicate subject and often confusing because of our very strong religious convictions. I would like to share with you an idea to contemplate. Just for a moment, take a deep breath, exhale, and completely relax.

Set aside all of your preconceived notions about this subject and read the following information as an objective observer.

Not one electron of energy is released from the Universal Source of all Life that is less than perfect. Therefore, everything that is manifesting in the physical realm that is less than perfect has to be a human creation.

Every world religion throughout history has agreed that the Earth is a schoolroom of learning. It is illogical to assume that we would come into the physical realm to spend our entire lives struggling and learning and then, at the end of that experience, die ,and that would be the end of it. What purpose could that possibly serve? In addition to the fact that it just plain wouldn't make any sense, we know that there is no way to destroy energy. We are energy; therefore, we are ongoing.

There are two schools of thought on what happens to us after we leave the physical plane. One school of thought is that as electronic energy passes through us into the physical plane, it remains part of the physical realm. Therefore, in order for us to have the opportunity to transmute our misqualified energy into harmony, we must be in the physical realm. The only way this could be accomplished is for us to return to the physical plane through re-embodiment. The second school of thought is that it is possible for us to still transmute our misqualified energy from another dimension, even though we may no longer be in a physical body. Consequently, we would continue our existence in the fourth dimension.

Regardless of which school of thought you ascribe to, the fact remains that we are responsible for every electron of precious life energy we use and, if we misqualify it, one way or another, it will keep returning to us to be transmuted back to its perfect state.

We have been drawn into the Earthplane from somewhere else, and at that time, we are the sum total of our thoughts, words, and deeds, and after we leave this plane, we will progress on to somewhere else and continue to be a sum total of every one of our life experiences.

I want to reiterate at this time that we must *never* judge another person by outer appearance. Many of these incoming children who are experiencing physical or mental problems are very strong, courageous lifestreams who have chosen a difficult experience in the physical plane so they can quickly transmute their misqualified energy and move on to their next octave of service free of that burden.

I have observed that whenever the subject is brought up of whether we re-embody on the Earthplane, there are extremely strong emotional feelings about it. I always find this a little bit amusing since no amount of debate is going to change the fact of whether we must return to the physical plane. I know at the present time this topic seems to be developing into a major issue and, instead of bringing any semblance of unity to the people on the planet, it is merely creating greater schisms and separation. Some orthodox religions are declaring the belief in re-embodiment to be "the work of the devil." Consequently, since three-fourths of the people on Earth believe in this possibility, millions are quite offended by that attitude. I personally feel this subject is being blown entirely out of proportion, and I would like to try to put it in perspective by projecting this thought: THE ONLY THING THAT MATTERS IS HERE AND NOW.

If it is true that we must return to the physical plane to transmute the energy we misqualified while in a physical body, that principle would then be natural law, which would mean that we are all subject to it, whether we believe it or not. If it is true that we do not return to the physical plane to transmute our misqualified energy, then that principle would be natural law and we would all be subject to it, whether we believe it or not.

In other words, there is no amount of belief or argument that is going to change the truth of this matter. If we do come back into embodiment, then we have all probably had thousands of lives; but what difference does that make to our responsibility at this very moment? I know many people who are desperately searching and trying to prove they have lived before. If it is true that we have lived before, we already messed up in that lifetime or we wouldn't be here today. So why waste our present life worrying about the past? I assure you that anything we need to know about our past will be filtered into our consciousness by our higher self when it is important for us to know. Otherwise, we are wasting our time in dwelling on the past, and that is a misqualification of energy.

To put this whole subject of whether we re-embody into perspective, I will venture to say, even without scientific proof, that we know for sure either we do or we don't! It's just that simple. If we do, we do, and if we don't, we don't. So let's stop worrying about it and get on with becoming the masters of our lives.

Now, back to the original point. I will state again that *NO INDIVIDUAL PERSON, PLACE, CONDITION, OR THING CAN RETURN OR INJECT ANYTHING INTO OUR PERSONAL EXPERIENCE WHICH WE HAVE NOT, IN THE FIRST INSTANCE, CREATED.* This is one of the most difficult natural laws to accept or comprehend, and yet, it is critical to attaining self-mastery.

The very positive side of this law is that since we have created the negative situations in our lives, by whatever means, we have the ability to do something about them. It was such a wonderful relief to me when I realized that there really wasn't a vengeful God sitting in the sky on His throne, arbitrarily messing up people's lives. If that were the case, what hope would we possibly have? Accepting responsibility removes the feeling of injustice or the "poor me" syndrome and changes us from the position of being victims of circumstance to the position of being creators of circumstance.

We must realize that this energy returns, not to plague us, but rather to give us the opportunity to change the vibration back to its original frequency. Remember, this is intelligent life energy that we have distorted and we are responsible for restoring it to perfection.

I would like to interject at this point that people often ask "What is perfection?" In this instance, perfection simply means returning this energy to its original vibration. This can be accomplished through the power of love. Love is one of the mightiest forces in the universe, and it is magnetic. There is no vibration that can resist or deny the power of love, or refuse to respond to love's call. Love can overcome hate, anger, loneliness, sadness, and all other misqualified feelings. Through understanding love, we can be in command of all the situations that arise in our lives.

In recent years, there has been a great deal of talk about love, some of it very emotional and superficial, some of it more scientific and meaningful. But we have really just begun to scratch the surface of the magnitude and power of this energy.

Accepting responsibility for our present life situation does not mean resignation or submission to the negative things that are taking place, but rather, it means developing a calm and detached attitude about them, recognizing each situation as an opportunity to transmute our misqualified energy and literally *love it free.* When we resent persons, places, conditions and things in our lives, it is usually because we have not understood the principle of natural law. Now that we realize, in actuality, we have created our present life situations by misqualifying energy through our thoughts, words, feelings, and actions, instead of rebelling when it is brought back to us through persons, places, conditions and things, we can look at these circumstances as opportunities to love our discordant energy back to its original vibration and, in fact, *be grateful.*

The more quickly we learn to transmute the negative circumstances of our lives back into the vibration of harmony through the power of love, the more quickly our lives will be the expressions of peace, harmony, love and happiness that we are longing for.

As I mentioned previously, this is not an easy concept to grasp. Because of our lifelong programming, it is common for us to look at the chaos in our lives and ask, "Why me?" We may be driving down the street and someone runs a red light and hits our car. From all outer appearances, we seem to be completely innocent. We may say to ourselves, "Of course it's true that I have been judgmental and critical all of my life, but what does that have to do with a car accident?" Our boss may come in and read us the riot act for no apparent reason. Our children may be causing us all kinds of problems. Our relatives and friends may be mean and hateful to us. We may become physically ill. We may lose our job or develop financial trouble of some other nature. We may be miserable in our marriage. We may fall down and break a leg. We may have mental problems and be anxious and confused. We may be robbed. Our house may burn down. We may be involved in a natural disaster of some sort, or any number of other things can go wrong. It is not important to know why these things are happening in our lives. We don't have to go back and dig up the past. It is self-defeating to blame or chastise ourselves. The only thing that matters is that we acknowledge that somehow, somewhere, sometime, we misqualified this energy and now natural law is returning it to us to give us the opportunity to love it free.

If we can maintain this attitude, it will greatly assist us in dealing with our negative life situations calmly and rationally. If we can truly understand that the persons, places, conditions and things that are being used to bring our misqualified energy back to us are just the tools or vehicles being used by natural law, this will allow us to be objective about the situation and not tie into it with more anger or resentment.

For instance, if we have a relative or a boss or any other person who is continually causing us problems, we should step back and look at the situation as an objective observer. We should acknowledge that it is not this person's fault. He or she is just the vehicle being used to return our own negative energy to us. If we get angry or upset with the person, it only compounds the problem. Then we have not only the original energy to transmute, but the additional anger as well. This additional anger will then go out from us again, accumulate more negative energy, and somehow it will be brought back to us at another time. As we can see, by responding negatively we have been creating quite a vicious circle for ourselves.

The process of *transmuting* the trials and tribulations of your life back into vibrations of harmony is accomplished in four easy steps. First of all, when negative circumstances occur, accept that this is merely your own misqualified energy returning to you for requalification. Regardless of how this energy is returned, when a negative situation occurs, consciously think to yourself, "This is my own negative energy returning to me. I am not going to get mad or upset at this person or condition because they are just being used as an instrument to return this energy to me. I am going to observe the situation objectively. I am going to remain centered and calm. I am going to handle this situation in the most constructive way possible, and I am going to love this energy back to its original vibration." The first step is *ACCEPTANCE*.

Then you must consciously thank the universe for the opportunity that has been provided for you to transmute this negative energy from discord to harmony. Say to yourself, "I give thanks to the universe, and I am grateful for the opportunity to love this energy free." The second step is *GRATITUDE*.

Next you must consciously ask for forgiveness for misqualifying the energy by saying, "I ask forgiveness for the misqualification of this precious gift of life. I ask forgiveness for all other life energy I have ever misqualified, both known and unknown, and I forgive myself for misqualifying this energy." The third step is *FORGIVENESS*. Forgiveness vibrates with the color of violet. Visualize violet light pouring through your heart into the situation at hand.

Then consciously send love into the situation. This is done

through creative visualization. In a later chapter we will discuss in detail the vibration and quality of color, but for now I will simply state that the color pink, in all of its hues, carries the vibration of love. So to send love into a circumstance, you need to ask the Universal Source of all Life to send forth the essence of pure love. Visualize this pink energy entering the top of your head and descending down into your heart's center, then project this pure pink love forth from your heart as a mighty laser beam of pink light into the negative energy returning to you, and say to yourself, "I am loving this negative energy *free*." The fourth step is *LOVE*.

This four-fold activity of acceptance, gratitude, forgiveness, and love creates an extremely powerful forcefield of constructive energy around you and, as the negative energy enters this forcefield, it is actually raised from a heavy, discordant frequency into a high, harmonious frequency.

This energy is electronic light substance and, as we increase the frequency of vibration from discord to harmony, it is the same as increasing the voltage of light in a dark room. Darkness cannot be sustained in the presence of light. Discord cannot be sustained in the presence of harmony.

Once this negative energy has been transmuted into positive energy again, it will continually remain a part of your overall constructive energy and magnetize good things into your life.

Through the process of deduction we can see that if we discipline ourselves and gain control of our thoughts, words, actions and feelings so that we are no longer misqualifying energy, and learn to handle the negative circumstances of our lives positively and constructively, transmuting the negative returning energy back into harmony, it will only be a matter of time until we no longer have negative energy returning to us, only our storehouse of good. At that point our lives will truly be transformed into expressions of joy and happiness.

This does not mean that there will no longer be negative things happening on the planet. Until everyone becomes master of his or her life, negativity will exist. But it means that our own individual world and our experiences will not reflect this negativity. This is known as *being in the world but not of the world*.

Then, through our example, we will be able to help our friends and loved ones attain peace in their own lives, and this knowledge of self-mastery will gradually be passed from one person to another until this entire planet is experiencing the Universal Oneness of all Life and living in peace. I know this sounds too good to be true, but it's happening at this very moment and you are a catalyst. I want to thank you for being here on Earth at this time and I want to thank you for being you.

Now I would like to look more deeply into the power of love so that it will really be a practical tool for you to use and not just an ephemeral thought.

In recent years, we have heard a great deal about unconditional love. Because of misunderstandings and half-truths, there has been a lot of "bad press" on this subject. I would like to state clearly that unconditional love does *not* mean allowing yourself to be a subservient, abused doormat. It does *not* mean that you should remain in a destructive relationship no matter what.

Unconditional love means allowing another person to be who they are and appreciating their uniqueness rather than demanding that they conform to your expectations.

At the present time, most people allow themselves to love another person conditionally. They agree to love someone on the condition that the person look the way they think the person should, or dress the way they think the person should, or have the "right" religious beliefs, the "right" skin color, the "right" nationality, the "right" job, the "right" social standing, the "right" political affiliations, and on and on.

All of this kind of love is crooked and through it we are cheating ourselves out of some of the most rewarding, fulfilling friendships imaginable.

The more we discover about this electronic energy that makes up all life, the more we become aware that what affects one part of life affects all life. This electronic Light permeates every part of life in the universe; consequently, we cannot have a negative thought without adding to the negative vibration of energy for the entire universe. We cannot have a positive thought without adding to the positive vibration of energy for the entire universe. *What affects one, affects all.*

Einstein spent his entire life trying to prove the Universal Field Theory, the interrelationship of all life—in actuality, the *Oneness of all Life.* If you will just contemplate that point for a moment, you will be able to see with a greater awareness how absolutely absurd it is to be prejudiced or to discriminate against any other part of life. To say you hate someone because of their race, religion, nationality, or anything else, is like saying you hate your hand, or you hate your arm, or you hate your leg. They are actually *part of you* and you cannot hurt them without hurting yourself. What a different place this planet will be when this truth finally registers in the consciousness of every man, woman and child living here.

We all know that there are many people participating in very objectionable behavior. Unconditional love does not mean that we should condone or support their destructive behavior, but it means that we should handle the destructive behavior in a constructive way and search for the positive characteristics in their personality and accentuate them. We should not hate these people, reject them, humiliate them or cast them aside to go out and do something else destructive. Whatever we put our attention and energy into we intensify; therefore, it is imperative that we learn to only intensify the positive behavior in another person.

From my observation, I think people demonstrate unconditional love most consistently with their children. Occasionally children do some really terrible things. Parents feel it is their responsibility to handle the situation, so they do, sometimes more calmly and constructively than others, but they do their best, according to their wisdom. Then they rebuild the child's sense of self-worth by pointing out the good qualities the child has to offer. Parents realize that these children are part of them and, therefore, how they behave is a reflection on them. So instead of just casting them aside and hating them or never speaking to them again, the parents strive to the best of their ability to help the children correct their problems and become constructive, worthwhile human beings.

This is the exact same attitude we need to develop toward everyone. If we will just realize that all people are a part of us, then we will be able to relate to them from a better perspective. We will be operating from a position of *how can I help myself*, rather than from a position of hate and rejection.

The best thing to do is to be a radiating example of unconditional love. The only way we ever teach anyone anything is through example. We can expound on the principle of love until we're blue in the face, but unless we are living, tangible proof of that law, all of our words will be to no avail.

First, we need to consciously create a forcefield of love around ourselves by drawing forth the vibration of acceptance, gratitude, forgiveness and love. This is accomplished by simply asking our higher selves to enfold us in this fourfold activity of love. Then feel yourselves being enveloped in the radiance of acceptance, gratitude, forgiveness and love. This forcefield has to be a deliberately maintained attitude of radiation. If we call it forth and then have a temper tantrum, we need to transmute that negative energy by applying the four simple steps of transmutation previously mentioned and then re-establish our forcefield of love.

The more proficient we become at sustaining this forcefield of love, the more harmonious our lives will be. When we are centered and balanced within this forcefield of love, we will be protected from tying into every negative situation that comes along with our anger or frustration. The more efficient we become at this, the more calmly and effectively we will be able to deal with our spouses, children, other family members, friends, co-workers, bosses, and associates. Rather than trying to function through the blinding eyes of emotion, we will be able to stand outside of the storm and operate as an objective observer.

This takes a great deal of discipline and practice, but it does work, once we learn to apply the law of love. Each day that we practice this law of love we will become more efficient, and soon it will be a natural part of our behavioral pattern.

It may seem amazing, but by changing the way we respond to the people in our lives, we can transform the entire relationship. It is very difficult to stay angry or continue to be nasty to someone if they are remaining calm and centered and responding to you with love. We have probably all experienced a situation in which we were extremely angry, and we may have even been ranting and raving at someone, but they remained calm and loving and, after a short time, we realized that we were making fools of ourselves.

We must accept that everyone has the right to be who they are; there is nothing we can do to *make* another person change. All we can do is change our own responses. But, almost miraculously, when we begin responding with love, the relationship will usually change from a source of tension or anger to a source of calm and peace.

Love is magnetic and also contagious. Remember that the power of love raises the discordant energy of hate, anger, frustration, anxiety, tension, or any other destructive emotion into a more harmonious vibration. So if we are radiating out enough love, we can actually change the atmosphere of our homes, offices, or environments into peaceful vibrations. This is not wishful thinking. This is a scientific natural law, and it is well worth our every effort to attain the discipline of the law of love. We can be *channels* for love by expanding our forcefield of love to engulf our homes, offices, neighborhoods, cities, states, countries, and planet.

In striving towards more harmonious relationships, one thing we must realize is that each and every person on this planet is going through the specific learning experiences that he/she personally needs for his/her own development and growth. Contrary to outer appearances or our own opinions, *all people are doing the very best they can with their lives, according to their understanding of the law.* Outer appearances are often very deceiving, and we never know just why another person is going through a particular life experience or behaving in a certain way. We must develop tolerance and patience in dealing with other people and, whenever possible, reveal to them the process of natural law so that, with a better understanding, they will perhaps take the steps necessary to get their lives in order. This does not mean preaching or interfering in any way with another's free will. It merely means being in tune with all life and, when the opportunity arises, to help another–*give them a drink from your cup.*

In reference to specific circumstances in our relationships, it is almost always possible to maintain harmony as long as we refuse to respond with anger, but there are occasions when another person insists of depriving us of our rights by abusing us physically, emotionally, or mentally. We are never obliged to remain in an abusive situation. The best thing for us to do is to remove ourselves from the situation and send love and forgiveness into that energy from a distance.

It is also possible to communicate with the higher self of that person. Our "higher self" is actually our super-conscious mind and this consciousness can be reached through the process of thought. We can actually speak to the higher self of another person with telepathic communication. All we have to do is think the name of the person or just think of the person and then ask the higher self of that person to take command and intervene on the destructive behavior and fill the person with illumination, wisdom and understanding so as to eradicate the self-defeating behavior.

This telepathic communication can be done at any time with our relationships. But remember: our higher selves operate only from the octaves of perfection, so don't ever try to manipulate anyone through this method. Our higher selves will only work to help us reach our highest potential, the good of our lifestreams.

In my counseling experience, I have found that by changing responses, a person can rekindle the love that was once in a marriage and restore the relationship to happiness. But occasionally, after much effort and discipline, one may become aware that, even though one partner is maintaining an atmosphere of love and harmony, the spouse is not adding to the joy of the marriage but is just existing. One then comes to a point of re-evaluation. A lack of friction is not everything in life. If it is obvious that one partner is putting 98 percent into a marriage and the spouse is putting only 2 percent in, it may be time to step back and determine if this is what is really wanted. Is this enough? Some people will say as long as they are living harmoniously and not fighting, it is enough. Others will say they want more sharing, a more fulfilling relationship, and decide this is not enough. This is a very individual choice, and each person should have the freedom to decide for him/herself.

The most complete expression I have found on the application of unconditional love is in one of the scrolls listed in Og Mandino's book *The Greatest Salesman in the World.* The scroll is titled "I Will Greet This Day With Love in My Heart," and I highly recommend that you obtain this book as part of your discipline toward self-mastery and read this particular scroll daily, striving with each breath to apply the principles of the law of love.

In conclusion, I would like to point out again that *what we put our attention on, we intensify and draw into our lives.* If we dwell on a particular personality trait, attitude, or behavior in another person that we find objectionable or offensive, we are actually compounding the problem and making it worse. The more we practice self-control and become a radiating center of love and peace, no matter where we are, the more cognizant we will be that our friends and loved ones are emulating more peace and calm in their behavior as well. It is possible to raise the awareness of all those around us by raising our own consciousness. Once we become the masters of love, we will reap tremendous rewards. We will realize that by tying into anger, resentment, frustration and hatred, we have been giving our power away and allowing other people to manipulate our emotions and control our lives.

With our new-found mastery of love, we will be able to interrelate with others much more effectively. We will be able to communicate rationally and share our thoughts and feelings. We will be able to recognize the choices in our relationships and make intelligent decisions. We will·be more receptive and able to release and let go of misconceptions. We will be more willing to compromise, and we will realize that two working together can draw perfection into this world much more quickly than one. We will ultimately experience happiness as a state of well-being that we can attain only by taking charge of our lives.

We have come to the point in the evolution of this planet when it is not enough just to be harmless. It is not enough to be negatively good, which means just ceasing to do wrong. It is time for us to put forth our energy into deliberately improving the quality of life, not only for ourselves, but for the rest of humanity as well.

The sea of energy we are living in permeates all life on this planet. With our every thought, word, action, or feeling, we are adding either to the Light of the world or to the darkness. As has been said before, *we are either part of the problem or part of the solution*. Let's be part of the solution.

By creating a forcefield of acceptance, gratitude, forgiveness and love, you can magnetize to yourself a life of happiness and fulfillment. The fact that you are reading this book means you still have hope that you can turn your life around. As long as you have hope, there isn't anything you can't accomplish.

I LOVE YOU!

6

The Secret of Financial Freedom

Because of the need for money in our everyday lives just for survival, we have developed a concern and tremendous fear about it that actually forms a block and repels money away from us. One of the most difficult things to truly believe and accept is that the supply of the universe is limitless and everything we need already exists. What we have to do is apply the natural laws that govern the abundant supply of the universe and open that flow into our lives.

In order to attain financial freedom, the first thing we must do is clear our relationship with money. We need to eliminate fear and realize that money is a source of energy, *period*. It is not some awesome entity that comes into our lives to wield its power over us and rule our destinies. It is only because of our fear that we have allowed money to have that control over us.

I am a counselor, and after observing the chaos going on in people's lives, some of my friends and I decided to offer a series of free classes to give people some tools to help them get in control of their situations. People had been hard hit by the economy, and many of them were in destitute financial plights. Some were having family problems and were on the verge of divorce, or their kids were giving them problems. A few were involved in drug or alcohol abuse. Others were struggling with a multitude of physical problems. Still others were having difficulty handling the stress of their jobs or other aspects of their lives, and several people were fighting off depression, boredom or a sense of plain hopelessness.

My friends and I printed flyers and distributed them throughout the city. We advertised the free classes in the newspaper and on the radio. From all outer appearances, you would logically think that a class of this nature being offered for free would draw a stampede of people seeking help, but it did not. In our first class, we had 12 people. We decided not to give up, so we offered the series of classes again and again. Slowly but surely, the classes began to grow, and friends recommended the series to other friends, and a feeling of trust developed. Now we have standing-room-only crowds and have given the class to several thousand people.

The point of sharing this story with you is that we asked for feedback from our students to help us improve the classes and meet their needs. Do you know what the greatest resistance and the largest concern was in attending the classes? *The fact that they were being offered for free!*

I think that is the most graphic example I can give you to demonstrate our fear of money. Here we were in the depths of one of the worst economic situations this country has ever known–skyrocketing inflation, unprecedented interest rates, record-setting unemployment–and yet people were afraid to take advantage of something that was being offered for free.

I heard all the typical cliches: "What's in it for you?" "What's the gimmick?" "You only get what you pay for." "Nobody gives away something for nothing." "If it's free, it must not be worth anything," etc. It was only after a great struggle on our part that people finally realized there really was no "catch," and the classes were being offered to them as a gift of love because people really *do care.*

A great deal of the fear and confusion we have about money comes from our childhood programming, from misunderstandings and religious dogma, as well as from our general feelings of low self-esteem or unworthiness. One of the most erroneous concepts we must let go of is the belief that it is *spiritual* or part of our *divine plan* to suffer and be poor. On the contrary, to say that our current state of disarray and lack is the "Will of God" is actually blasphemous.

Since not one electron of energy is sent forth from the Universal Source of all Life that is less than perfect, it follows that *poverty*, which is most certainly less than perfect, has to be part of our own human creation. Therefore, poverty is not only not the Will of God but, since it is a form of misqualified energy, it could actually be considered in religious terms as a *sin*. It is a vice. Poverty leads to all manner of crime, family problems, drug and alcohol abuse, tension, stress, high blood pressure, worry, and numerous other physical and mental problems. There is nothing righteous about it. So, first and foremost, we must accept that *poverty is not a virtue*. Acceptance of this truth will help us let go of all of the previous programming with which we have been inflicted that has made us feel guilty about attaining prosperity.

The next thing we need to look at is our self-image. Often, the feelings of unworthiness, which we usually take on at a very early age, convince us that we don't deserve to have the good things in life. We usually have difficulty imagining ourselves financially prosperous, or imagining ourselves in the most wonderful circumstance possible. Somehow we just don't feel worthy of happiness. I want to state emphatically that such belief is a lie. It is a misqualification of pure energy. We need to get in touch with those feelings, recognize them for what they are, and let them go. We must begin loving ourselves more, appreciating our uniqueness, recognizing our gifts and talents, and accepting that we each have a special service we can offer this planet, and the time to start using it is now. We should love ourselves enough to give ourselves what we truly deserve–*the very best*.

We can do a lot more good and help many more people if

we have money than we can if we're poor. Money doesn't have to be an instrument of selfishness or greed. Instead, it can be a tool to expand our love and our gifts to the rest of the world. Since we usually use pain as our motivator, it is during our failures and our miserable periods that we develop the incentive to look for a better way and finally become willing to apply the natural laws of prosperity. From all outer appearances, I think we're miserable enough. Let's apply the laws of prosperity *now* and draw the limitless abundance of the universe into our lives.

Now that we have identified some of the reasons we may have chosen to hold ourselves in a state of financial limitation, we can let go of those concepts of negative thinking and begin developing a consciousness of prosperity. Prosperity thinking basically gives us the power to make our dreams come true, whether those dreams are concerned with increased wealth, better health, a happier personal life, more education, career success, a deeper spiritual life, or anything else we desire. We are prosperous to the degree that we are experiencing peace, health and plenty in our worlds.

Failure is due to failure thinking. "As a man thinketh in his heart, so he is." Author James Allen said, "Through his thoughts, man holds the key to every situation, and contains within himself that transforming, regenerative agency by which he may make of himself what he wills." This an extremely powerful statement. The laws that govern prosperity are just as sure and workable as the laws that govern mathematics, music, physics and every other field of science.

We have concluded that every single thing existing in this universe is composed of electronic light substance. There are two activities of this electronic substance. One is *radiation*, which means projecting forth or sending out. The other is *magnetization*, which means pulling back or drawing in. Familiar phrases used to describe these two activities are "giving and receiving," "cause and effect," "action and reaction," "sowing and reaping," and "supply and demand," in actuality the Law of the Circle.

The basic Law of Prosperity is identical. What we radiate out through our thoughts, feelings, mental pictures, words and actions, we magnetize into our lives and affairs. If we are sending out thoughts and feelings of lack and limitation, bogged down with memories of unpleasant failure experiences, and worry or concern over not being able to pay our bills, or the fear that we won't have money to purchase our bodily needs, that misqualified energy, charged with the vibration of poverty, is what we will be drawing into our lives and sustaining in our lives.

It is up to us to *dare* to radiate outward through our thoughts, feelings and actions what we really want to experience in life rather than dwell on what we're afraid of and what we don't want to experience.

These negative conditions in our lives can change as quickly as we change our thinking about them. We have all heard the expression "money begets money." That is true because people who have money have developed true prosperity consciousness. They accept prosperity, they feel prosperous, they send out thoughts of prosperity, and they continually draw success and prosperity into their lives. I know it is a whole lot easier to think and feel and act prosperous when we have money than when we don't, but the important thing is that it is possible, and it is something we *must* learn to do if we are going to attract prosperity into our lives.

Every time we send money out, whether it is to buy groceries, to pay a bill, for entertainment, or whatever, we should bless it with gratitude for the service it is providing to us and let it go freely, knowing that it is a source of energy and, like all energy, it will go out, expand, and return to us for more service. If we send our money forth grudgingly, bemoaning the high cost of living, fearing we won't have enough to cover our expenses, hating to spend it on the necessities of life, we will automatically block the flow of the universe from pouring into our lives. This does not mean going out and charging things and spending money we don't have, but it does mean recognizing money as a *source of energy* that is providing a service to us that we should accept with gratitude and appreciation.

It is important for us to take our attention off poverty and be deliberate about wealth. Our thoughtforms are magnetic. Through persistence, confidence, and acceptance, we can draw the universal supply of all good things into our lives. Through the steps of creative visualization, we can set our goal of prosperity and begin developing true prosperity consciousness.

Imagine that you just won a million-dollar lottery. Feel the elation and buoyancy of prosperity. Experience the feeling of success. Now visualize all the things you would do with that money. Visualize yourself going to the bank and depositing your check. See yourself joyously paying off all your debts and absorb that feeling of *freedom.*

Visualize yourself now buying the things you have wanted and needed. See yourself helping friends and loved ones who need assistance. Visualize yourself now as you invest your money wisely so that it will grow and expand and continue to serve you.

Experience happiness and the sense of fulfillment as you use your money not only to add to the joy of your own life but to improve life for others on the planet as well.

Even though you may not win a million-dollar lottery, it is this feeling of success and abundance that you must generate in order to create a magnetic forcefield to draw prosperity into your life. Hold on to that feeling of buoyancy and joy and feel that prosperity continually throughout the day. Don't give power to the outer-world appearances by dwelling on lack and limitation. Handle the situations in your life as an objective observer, knowing always that regardless of what is occurring at this moment in your life, the supply of the universe is limitless and abundance is on its way to you.

Now I want to share with you another very important factor

in attaining financial freedom. As I have stated, the two-fold activity of the universe is radiation and magnetization, give and take. When working with natural law, there must always be a balance. For every cause, there is an effect, and for every action, there must be a reaction. The universe has given us our gift of life, the electronic Light Substance that beats our physical hearts and allows us to think, move, breathe, and live in the physical plane. In addition to that, the universe has provided everything we need to survive on earth. We have the sun, water, air, food, and material for clothing and shelter. We have chosen to live in a society, so we use money to purchase our bodily needs at the present time, but even without money, the universe has already provided everything we need to exist on this planet.

This is our gift of life and we have accepted it, used it, and benefited from it. Now we must give something back to the universe in return for our gift of life. This is the natural give-and-take of the universe; when we comply with this law, we open ourselves up to unlimited abundance.

What is happening at the present time is that we are spending our money on the basics that the universe has already provided for free, such as food, water, clothing, shelter, etc. In order to activate the limitless flow of abundance, it is not enough for us to just give the minimum of energy in the form of money back to the universe to pay for the things that have already been given to us for free. If we simply give money to pay for the services that the universe has already provided, it is like not giving back anything at all and, consequently, we hold ourselves in a pattern of lack and limitation and only draw to ourselves the minimum we need to survive.

The secret of financial freedom is to give back to the universe, in loving gratitude, more energy or money than we spend on our bodily needs. This does not mean just spending more money on things we want or enjoy, but rather, it means giving money back to the universe in gratitude and appreciation for our gift of life. In just writing that statement I can already feel the resistance and hear the laments, "I don't even have money to cover my bills. How do you expect me to give money away?"

That is just that old entity "fear" cropping up. Just for a moment set it aside and read the following information with an open mind. The application of this natural law is the key to your financial freedom.

I will state again: the natural law of the universe is give-and-take. The universe has given and we have taken. The universe has given us life and we have accepted it in the form of electronic energy, light, air, water, food, clothing and shelter. Now, being subject to natural law, we must give something back to the universe. The fact that we have accepted this gift of life from the universe and have chosen to be in a physical body means that, on a higher level, through our super-conscious mind, we understand about this law of give-and-take, and we have agreed to it. If we had refused to accept this gift of life, knowing that we were going to have to give something back in return for it, we simply would not have been allowed to come into the physical plane. Obviously, we are here, so we agreed to accept that gift. In other words, "we have danced to the music, and now it's time to pay the fiddler."

Throughout history, world religions have been trying to get this fact across to us by having us "tithe," which means giving a tenth of our income to the church. In my personal experience, the reasons for tithing were never explained clearly enough, and there was always so much pressure from the head of the church that it never seemed like a free-will gift, given in loving gratitude, but rather just another bill we had to pay. Because of that attitude, tithing usually doesn't have the effect of opening the prosperity flow. The attitude, motive, and spirit with which we give this money back to the universe is the most important thing about our gift. Our motivation *must* be that *this money we are giving away is a gift of love we are giving back to the universe in gratitude and appreciation for our gift of life.*

We can give this gift of money or energy back to the universe in a multitude of different ways. Remember, there's no mocking natural law; so this gift must always work for the betterment of the planet, absolutely no strings attached. If we give this money to our children so that it won't be too far away from us, and it will still be in the family, that doesn't count. If we give it to someone to manipulate them and make them feel obligated to us, that doesn't count. If we give it to the dealers in Las Vegas or for any other gamble that we're expecting to win a bundle on, that doesn't count. We must give the money away expecting nothing in return from the person, place, or thing we give it to. But the wonderful thing about this gift is that money is energy, and, when we send energy out, it expands and returns to us greatly magnified over what we originally sent out. Even though we expect nothing in return from the person, place, or thing we give our money to, we *do* expect something in return from the universe.

The general rule that has been applied throughout time is that if we will give as little as ten percent of our wealth back to the universe in gratitude for our gift of life, we will have such a flow of abundance into our lives that we won't be able to handle it all. This ten percent is not part of our cost of living; it is a love offering for our gift of life.

If we stop and think for a moment, we give waiters and waitresses a fifteen percent gratuity. Is it too much to ask to give ten percent for our gift of life?

Whom we choose to give our money to should be our decision. We should not allow ourselves to be pressured into giving our money to things we don't fully support. That interferes with our ability to believe this is our gift to the universe and it blocks our flow.

Our money can be given to spiritual institutions, organizations that we feel are teaching people how to improve the quality of their lives, scientific research, universities and learning institutions, organizations for music and the arts, charities, needy families, or any other constructive activity that we would like to support.

For those of you who are still experiencing resistance and feeling "there is no way I can possibly afford to do that," understand that *we don't have any choice in the matter*. We have already accepted our gift of life and now we *must* give something back to the universe *in one way or another*. It is natural law.

Unfortunately, because of our lack of understanding about this law, the large majority of people are giving this energy back through drudgery and suffering and the sweat of their brows, working long, difficult hours for a meager existence. This agony is one way of giving energy back to the universe, but it is certainly not the best way or the most enjoyable way, and by no means is it the most constructive way. Even though we may have made this choice to remain in a state of drudgery at a subconscious level, it was still our own free-will choice. Consequently, we have the absolute free will to change our method of repayment to the universe.

In order to open the flow of unlimited abundance into our lives, we must freely give money back to the universe for things other than just covering the expenses of our bodily needs. The most painless way, and the most profitable way, is a method I'll refer to as *seed money.* An excellent book on this subject is titled *Seed Money in Action: Working the Ten-Fold Law of Return* by Jon P. Speller. Seed money is money we deliberately give back to the universe, knowing that it will expand at least ten-fold on its return to us. This is money we give away to any activity, organization, institution, or person of our choice, with no strings attached, expecting nothing in return from them but accepting that the natural law of the universe will expand that money at least ten-fold on its return to us. It's important that we understand clearly that we don't expect anything from the recipient of our money, but we *do* expect the flow of abundance from the Universal Source of all Life.

To activate this flow of abundance, we need to consciously put our attention into it with our thoughts, words, feelings and actions. We need to know and accept that this is a scientific law. As we give our money away in loving gratitude for our gift of life, *we must consciously claim our ten-fold return*. As an example, if we give $100 away, we must consciously say, "I have received $1,000 with the good of all concerned," accepting beyond a shadow of a doubt that that money is on its way back to us. When we say "with the good of all concerned," we eliminate the possibility of negative inter- ference. We must never be willing to attain prosperity at the expense of anyone else. This will tragically backfire in our faces. I know from outer appearances that it seems as though many people have attained great wealth by being dishonest and stepping on people along the way. But I assure you that we cannot take anything away from someone else without something being taken away from us. We have often heard that people spend the first 40 years of their lives acquir- ing their fortunes and the next 40 years spending the fortunes trying to regain their health. That is a graphic example of the accuracy of the law when the wealth is acquired by unethical means.

After we have claimed our ten-fold return, we must feel gratitude for that gift. Gratitude opens the door to abundance and it's an indispensable catalyst for our ten-fold return.

It is imperative that we not worry about where the money will be coming from. By putting our attention and concern into where the money could possibly come from, we actually limit ourselves and set up blocks. We must just accept, be- lieve, know, and feel that the money is flowing back to us in accordance with natural law.

In the book *Seed Money in Action* by Speller, and in another excellent book, *The Dynamic Laws of Prosperity*, by Catherine Ponder, many success stories and examples are given on how accurate this natural law is. The examples prove that our re- turn can come from totally unexpected sources. Just re- member that with seed money the ten-fold return *is expected*, the means of that return *is unexpected*. Through the proper ap- plication of this law, our prosperity is assured and can be limited only by our lack of constancy. The supply of the universe is limitless and its flow into our lives has been blocked only by our own misapplication of the law.

If you are currently having trouble making ends meet, I know it is difficult to even think of giving away ten percent of your income, but, if you are going to get out of the situation, you have to begin somewhere. If you can really accept that for every $10 you give away you will receive $100 in return, *which is the truth of the law,* then it will make it easier to let go. You can begin by giving away $5 or $10 here and there, claiming your ten-fold return each time. Then, with courage, give away more and more until you begin to experience the wonderful flow of prosperity.

There are a few questions that always come up on this subject, so I will answer them now. One question is, "If I don't have any money to give away, can I give away my services or my time or something else?" It is certainly better to give away something rather than nothing, but the law is *like attracts like.* So if we want to attract money into our lives, we need to give money away. Do the best you can. As soon as you can start giving it away, do it, even if you start with only a dollar.

Another question is, "Does it count if I claim this gift as a deduction on my income tax?" There is nothing wrong with claiming this deduction on your income tax as long as that was not your reason for giving the gift. If you did it *only* for a tax writeoff, then, of course, it doesn't count as a love offering for your gift of life.

Another question is, "I feel guilty giving this money as a gift of love and then expecting a ten-fold return. Are you sure this is fair?" This is not only fair, it is part of our gift of life that we have been refusing to accept, actually rejecting. These feelings of guilt stem from our old programming of believing that somehow it's spiritual to be poor, or that it's not "right" to want money. We keep hearing the statement, "Money is the root of all evil." That is not what the Bible says at all. The statement is "The *worship* of money is the root of all evil," which is quite a different matter.

It is time for us to sweep away the misconceptions that we have clung to in the past and begin our new pattern of prosperity consciousness. This can be accomplished by controlling our thoughts, setting goals, visualizing creatively, affirming positively, and giving seed money away so we can claim our ten-fold law of return and draw the abundant supply of the universe into our lives.

Our Financial Freedom is possible now. Let's go for it!

I AM PROSPERITY

1. *I let go of the misconception that anyone or anything can withhold from me all that this abundant universe has for me now.*

2. *Since I Am one with all life in this universe, I share in the limitless supply of all good things.*

3. *I Am a channel for all kinds of riches to flow to me now.*

4. *I Am an irresistible magnet with the power to draw to myself the supply of all good things according to the thoughts, feelings and mental pictures I continually hold in my consciousness.*

5. *I realize that I Am responsible for my life situation, and I have the power to create whatever I wish in my life. As of this moment, I choose to create for myself a life of health, success, happiness, and prosperity.*

6. *I know that this universe is filled with perfect abundance and I accept these riches into my life now. I choose lavish abundance for myself and for all mankind.*

7. *I know all of my needs will be perfectly met at all times.*

8. *Rapid changes come in all aspects of my life as I open my mind to the unlimited resources of this universe now.*

9. *All of my financial affairs are in perfect order now.*

10. *I love doing my work, and I am richly rewarded, both creatively and financially.*

11. *I give my love, my gifts, my all, and I Am therefore rich, well, and happy now.*

I AM PROSPERITY

7

Healing and Maintaining the Health of Our Physical Bodies

Our physical bodies are truly the most wonderful instruments in the universe. In this chapter, we're going to learn how to apply the mental aspects of healing in a practical, effective manner, and how to accelerate the natural healing process of the body by cooperating with the laws of nature that govern us.

Initially, it is important for us to understand just what causes our physical bodies to malfunction or become diseased in the first place. Every cell and organ of our physical bodies is composed of electronic energy, molecules, atoms, electrons, neutrons, protons, etc. When we are in a perfect state of health, the electronic substance of our bodies is vibrating at a very high frequency of harmony. In this state, we have a natural immunity that is invulnerable. When our bodies are vibrating at this high frequency, the cell membranes are strong and diseases of all kinds are deflected. Then our natural immune system takes over and consumes the destructive organisms. We all fight off cancer cells, bacteria, viruses, and various other forms of disease every single day. It is only when there is an imbalance or discordant frequency of vibration within the cells of our bodies that our cell membranes become weak and disease can penetrate the cells and take hold.

To get a clearer picture of this process, we can visualize the propeller of an airplane. If the propeller is immobile or rotating very slowly, we can easily hold onto the blades, but, if the rotation is increased to full speed, we will be cast aside through centrifugal force and deflected.

To heal the physical body, we must learn what causes the body to develop a discordant frequency of vibration, and then what steps can be taken to accelerate the vibration back to its perfect state of immunity. To understand this process, we must again look to the Law of the Circle. When the electronic energy from the Universal Source is allowed to pass through the body harmoniously, there is no interference in the vibratory action of the cells and organs and, in fact, as this energy goes out and accumulates additional harmonious energy along the way and then returns to us with greater momentum than we originally sent out, this returning flow of constructive energy penetrates the body and works as an accelerator to increase the vibration of the cells and organs to an even higher frequency.

Unfortunately, when we intercept this flow of energy from the Universal Source and change the vibration from its perfect frequency of harmony into discordant mutations of hatred, anger, frustration, fear, etc., exactly the opposite happens. Recall that in Chapter 5 we discussed the cohesive power of love. This is the same frequency that vibrates as the magnetic center of the atom. An atom smasher, with all its powerful, dynamic pressure, releases the electrons in one atom, but, when we have an emotional outburst, that destructive energy explodes through the cells and organs of our physical bodies like an atom bomb and literally shatters the magnetic poles within the atoms that make up the cells of our bodies.

As we proceed through life setting off these atomic explosions in our physical bodies, the atomic structure gradually becomes weaker and our cells begin to disintegrate, enabling all manner of disease to take hold. Then, to compound the problem, this destructive energy accumulates additional negative energy and returns to us, bombarding us again with heavy, discordant vibrations. When this negative energy returns to us and passes through the cells of our bodies, it is like putting our fingers in a fan. Our bodies are vibrating at a particular frequency, this discordant barrage of energy enters our bodies, the electrons begin slowing down and wobbling on their axes, and their vibrations become distorted.

The more we are discovering–or I should say understanding–about the Law of Life, the more we are becoming aware that every atom in the body revolves around a core of love that is affected by every emotion. Negative emotions set these atoms off center and cause them to become weak and distorted. Harmonious, positive energy strengthens the magnetic centers, prevents disintegration, and brings harmony and health.

For quite some time the medical world has known that the mental attitude of a patient is critical to the healing process, and in certain cases, even to the survival of the patient. With a greater understanding of natural law, the reasons for this become quite obvious.

A study was done at the University of California at Los Angeles with cancer patients to find out why some people respond so much better to treatment than others. At first it was thought that some patients naturally did well because their disease was not as severe, but on closer scrutiny, it was discovered that the severity of the illness was only one of a number of factors that accounted for the differences between those who recovered and those who did not. It was discovered that there were certain major characteristics among the survivors.

These factors were:
1. They all had a strong will to live.
2. They were not panicky about their illness.
3. They had confidence in their ability to persevere.
4. Despite all of the forecasts to the contrary, they believed they could make it.
5. They were capable of joyous response.
6. They were convinced that their treatment would work.

In 1977 a Nobel Prize was granted in the field of medicine for research done in the mental aspects of healing. It was discovered that joy and happiness, as well as laughter, cause electrical impulses in the brain that release hormones that enhance our natural immune system. Conversely, anger, resentment and hatred cause the release of hormones that suppress our natural immune system. It has also been found that tears from laughter, tears from grief, and tears from peeling onions have entirely different chemical compositions.

The incredibly exciting part of our greater awareness of natural law is that, even though, through a lack of understanding, we may have done things in the past that attributed to the current state of *"dis-ease"* in our physical body, we now have the practical tools available to help us correct the situation. The importance of understanding our responsibility in the breakdown of our natural immune system is certainly not to instill blame or guilt, but rather to help us understand that disease is a human creation, and, therefore, we as human beings have the power to do something about it.

I would like to share with you now some detailed information that will help you apply the natural resources available to all of us that will accelerate the healing process. This information is *not* intended to take the place of sound medical assistance, but it can easily be incorporated with any treatment you are presently taking. I want to stress this point of *sound medical assistance*. Many times people feel that because some people have completed medical school and have an "M.D." next to their names, they must be "all knowing." Doctors of all degrees are fallible, and we owe it to ourselves to be perceptive and discerning in choosing with whom we would like to entrust our well being. We need to keep abreast of the times and informed about new research, techniques and methods of treating our particular affliction, so that when a type of treatment is suggested to us, we can make an educated decision.

To begin our journey back to vibrant health and vitality, we must expand our self-awareness. For a greater understanding of just how our thoughts, words, and actions affect our health, we should realize that we are working with four different energy fields. These energy fields are vehicles that we use to navigate around in the physical plane. For our purposes here, I am going to call them our four *lower bodies*. We have a dense *physical body* which we can all see and are very aware of. This is the body which may malfunction and become diseased. We have an *etheric body* which is more refined and less dense. This etheric body is identical to the physical body and extends a little beyond the physical form. It is composed of four chemical ethers. This energy field has been photographed with Kirlian photography. The radiance of the etheric body is what is being called the aura. We have an etheric counterpart to each cell and organ of the physical body. When someone has a limb amputated, what is known as "phantom pain" is occasionally experienced. This occurs because the etheric portion of that limb still remains and has a degree of sensation. Gradually, as time passes, the ethers will dissipate without the support of the physical limb, and the pain will cease. The ethers of the etheric body are extremely sensitive and record every single thought, word, or action we have ever expressed. This body is known as the core of all of our memories because it continually records every one of our life experiences. The third lower vehicle is our *mental body*. This body is our link of mind into the world of thought. Our mental body enables us to think and projects thoughtforms into the physical brain structure. Our mind and the process of thought are different from our physical brain structure. Our physical brain is merely the instrument we use to bring our thoughts into the physical realm. Just as we are not our physical body, but rather our body is merely the vehicle we use to move around in the physical plane, our brain is not our mind or mental body, but rather the vehicle our mind uses to channel thoughts into the physical plane. Our fourth vehicle is the *emotional body*. This is the energy field through which we express all of our feelings and emotions. This body is the largest of our four lower bodies, and the greatest amount of our life energy is released through this vehicle. Up to 80 percent of all of the energy we expend is released through our emotions. The other 20 percent of our energy is released through our other three bodies: physical, etheric or mental.

Our physical body is comprised of 80 percent water, and so is our emotional body. It is for this reason that unusual things happen to people during a full moon. Scientifically, we know that the full moon has a powerful effect on the water element. The additional gravitational pull during a full moon affects the tides of the ocean and the water element in our physical and emotional bodies as well. If we are balanced and centered, the additional energy field of the full moon can have an extremely constructive effect on us, but if we are a little out of balance or off center, that additional pressure on the emotional body can make us go beserk and do weird things. The newspapers are always filled with reports of increased crime during the full moon. It is because of this phenomenon that the words lunacy and lunatic were coined, as a derivative from the Latin *luna*, meaning moon.

The importance of knowing about these four lower vehicles is that an imbalance in any one of them can eventually result in the illness or disease of our physical body.

At the present time, the medical world is declaring as much as 80 percent of all illness to be psychosomatic. Many people think this means the illness is all in the head or imaginary, but that is not what psychosomatic means at all. A psychosomatic illness is a bodily disorder or malfunction that *is induced by mental or emotional disturbances.* This does not mean it is all imagination, but rather, it is a physical illness that has been created through the misuse of thoughts and feelings.

This is a very complicated subject, and we have truly just begun to scratch the surface of discovering the effects of our thoughts and feelings on the health of our physical body, but we seem to be proving more and more that *"as a man thinketh in his heart, so he is."* What we hold in our consciousness, we begin to manifest in our physical body. In my field of counseling, I work specifically with helping people accept responsibility in the healing process of their bodies. Far too many times I have seen the symptoms of an illness subside with medical treatment only to recur a short time later. We can treat symptoms forever and temporarily achieve a semblance of relief, but, if we don't correct whatever it is that caused the malfunction of our immune system and allowed the illness to take hold of our bodies, it will continue to recur. To attain vibrant health, it is imperative that we evaluate our illness and try to discover just why our physical bodies became susceptible to disease.

Each of us individually is responsible for the health of our body, and only we can accurately determine what has occurred in our lives that affected us so intensely that we allowed the breakdown of our physical body as a result of it. In most instances, this is certainly not a deliberate or a conscious decision on our part, but through the process of natural law, it is the end result.

As a counselor, it is not my job to tell people what they are doing wrong but merely to function as a catalyst in helping them to the point of realization through their own self-awareness.

My patients and I together have discovered many very interesting things about the manifestation of disease. This may seem like an oversimplification, and I am in no way suggesting that this is true in every case, but many times we have observed that the malfunction of the physical body is due to years of persistant negative attitudes, fears, prejudices and beliefs. The possibilities of this occurrence are legion, but I would like to share with you some of the more common examples.

I have worked with people who have developed cataracts, and upon analysis, they will come to the conclusion that for years they were offended by the negative things going on in their lives, and just plain didn't like what they saw. Subconsciously, they were sending their body messages indicating, "I don't like what I'm seeing, and I don't want to see this anymore." Eventually their bodies believed that message and began co-operating by closing off the path of vision. Cataracts, of course, can be surgically treated, but, if the attitude is not corrected, they will grow back.

A similar affliction can occur with hearing. A perpetual attitude of, "I don't want to hear that anymore," will gradually register in the intelligence of the body, and it will co-operate by blocking the ability to hear.

The Heart Chakra, which we will discuss in more detail in a later chapter, is a vortex of energy through which we channel love into the physical plane. This chakra has a powerful effect on the physical heart, and often, if people are having difficulty or are unable to express or receive love freely, they can block off the flow of energy through this Heart Chakra and create a gradual blockage in the physical heart system as well, thus creating varying degrees of malfunction in the heart.

I have observed people who are bitter and angry or resentful, refusing to partake of the "sweetness of life," develop malfunctions of the pancreas, creating hypoglycemia or sugar diabetes.

Often people who have difficulty experiencing security or stability in their lives, or who lack structure, begin to develop problems with the foundation or structure of their physical bodies, as in bones, joints, or muscles.

It is not unusual for people who have a fear of interrelating with other people to develop severe skin problems, or obesity, so as to try and make themselves offensive to others in order not to have to deal with personal relationships.

I have also worked with people who are egotistical and arrogantly power oriented. They develop problems with their Throat Chakra, which is our power center and corresponds to the thyroid gland. These people often have goiters or other thyroid problems.

Many times people who are critical or judgmental or abuse the power of speech in other ways develop pyorrhea or other oral disorders.

People who have various difficult situations going on in their lives to the extent that they are "fed up" or "can't stomach any more" will begin to manifest all manner of digestive and stomach disorders.

On occasion I have worked with terminally ill patients who have decided life is not worth living and have chosen what they consider to be a sociably acceptable means of suicide. If we poison ourselves, or jump off a cliff, or hold a gun to our heads, we create a barrage of guilt and resentment in our loved ones. But, if we create a terminal illness, we accomplish the same end result without any blame or hard feelings, or so it seems. Again, there is no mocking natural law, and to do so is a gross misqualification of pure energy.

I have given the preceding examples, not to accuse or blame, and certainly not so that we can try to figure out anyone else's problems, but merely to give us food for thought. As I mentioned, these circumstances clearly do not exist in every case of the aforementioned diseases, but for us to really get to the core of our problem, we need to be completely honest in our evaluation. The more insight we have into our illness, the more effective we can be in attaining a *permanent* healing.

In understanding natural law, we must realize that only perfection is sent forth from the Universal Source of all Life.

Anything less than perfect health is, therefore, a human creation. Consequently, disease in all of its forms is self-inflicted through one means or another. I feel confident in saying the majority of diseases are caused by the misapplication of the law of harmony through negative patterns of thought, opinions, attitudes, beliefs, and feelings. Through scientific research, we have discovered that, when the sentiments of envy, hate, fear, anger, and resentment are habitual emotions in the body, they are capable of starting organic changes that actually result in genuine disease. Scientists have stated that there is mind power in every cell, and each cell is filled with life, light, intelligence, and substance which forms our atomic structure. When we continually send destructive messages to the intelligence within these cells, they begin to obey our command and eventually outpicture our distorted programming.

In order to restore the physical body back into an instrument of vibrant health, we need to thoroughly evaluate our thinking patterns and attitudes. After we have pinpointed the problem, we can then take the necessary steps to change our destructive habits and begin drawing perfect health into every cell, organ, and function of our bodies.

The first step in the healing process is to stop our destructive habits. We need to observe and monitor what is going on in our four lower bodies and strive, through self-discipline, to eliminate negative habits that are self-defeating. For example, every function of the physical body, whether we are talking about our ability to think, move, speak, digest food, breathe, produce blood, restore cells, heal ourselves, or whatever, is a direct result of certain chemical reactions. If the proper chemicals are not present in the form of vitamins, minerals, trace minerals, cell salts, etc., then the body cannot produce the proper hormones, enzymes, or cells to allow the body to efficiently perform its specific tasks. Since our physical bodies are such magnificent instruments, they will compensate for the vitamin and mineral deficiencies for quite some time, but eventually, they will no longer be able to bear the extra burden, and a malfunction will occur, resulting in some form of physical illness or disease.

Each one of us individually has the responsibility of supplying the proper chemicals to our body. If we want to remain in a state of optimum health, we must learn what our body needs and how we can best fulfill those needs. The purpose of this chapter, however, is not to give a lesson in nutrition; health food stores are filled with excellent books on this subject that will help you establish a program for yourself. The general rule is: the purer the food and the closer it is to its natural state when we consume it (in other words, the less processing it has been through) the more nutritious it is, and the less stress it causes on the physical body. That is a very important factor in the process of healing. Our physical body needs proteins, fats, and carbohydrates, as well as vitamins, minerals and water. These elements come in a variety of forms, and for us to determine just what form is best for our body may take a little time and concentration. It is important for us to educate ourselves and seek the guidance of a competent, *nutritionally trained* doctor, but I assure you that if you want to stop the degenerative process of your physical body and achieve buoyant health, it is well worth your every effort.

While we are in the processes of learning about our own individual needs, we can begin our return to health by getting plenty of fresh air, exercise, and improving our diet. We can improve our diet by consuming a wide variety of fresh fruits and vegetables, nuts and seeds, whole grains, pure dairy products, natural oils, and pure water. It will also help to eliminate highly processed, refined foods that have been stripped of their nutritional value. Many of these foods are just "empty" calories.

When we get to the point of deciding whether or not we need to supplement our diet with additional vitamins and minerals, we must decide if it is better to use synthetic or natural vitamins. There is quite a controversy going on about this subject and depending on with whom we are speaking, we will get entirely different opinions. There are scientists and nutritionalists who claim there is absolutely no difference between synthetic and natural vitamins, and, if we are speaking about one isolated chemical composition, that is probably true. For instance, synthetic vitamin B6 and the isolated natural B6 are chemically the same, but in nature B6 does *not* occur in an isolated state, but rather with the entire B-complex vitamins in their proper balance to ensure the most effective reaction in the body. Our body does not need just one, or two, or three of the B vitamins in an isolated form, but rather it needs all of the B-complex in proper balance. If we take a natural B-complex vitamin, which is actually just concentrated food, we get the whole complex as it naturally occurs, and we don't risk the imbalances of taking concentrated doses of one, or even a few, of the B vitamins.

In addition to the above reason for taking natural vitamins, the science of nutrition is relatively new, and, as we learn more about it, we are discovering greater and greater complexities in the chemical composition of food. There are factors we haven't even identified in our food that we may find are critical to the proper assimilation and function of vitamins and minerals in the body. These factors are missing in synthetic vitamins and minerals.

I don't want to give the impression that synthetic vitamins don't serve a purpose, because they clearly do. In certain deficiencies, we need megadoses of a certain vitamin of which we could not possibly obtain the concentrated amount if we were taking just natural vitamins. These megadoses should *always* be taken under the direction of a nutritionally trained doctor and not on our own. But, because of the reasons I have mentioned, if we are simply attempting to supply our body with the necessary chemicals it needs to function efficiently that we may not be getting in our food, it is best to take natural vitamins which are just concentrated food.

We need to apply *all* of the factors of good health if we are to attain a vibrant state of health. We may be physically supplying our body with the correct balance of nutrition, but, if we are still bombarding it with negative thoughts, feelings or memories, our nutritional efforts will be to no avail. So, in addition to proper care of our physical body, we need to be cognizant and in control of our thoughts, words, and actions. We must be deliberate about health. We know that whatever we put our attention and energy into we intensify. Therefore, it is critical for us to stop giving power to the disease through our fear and worry.

For instance, we think of cancer as a powerful entity that comes in and ravages our body. Actually, cancer cells are very weak, confused cells and can *only* take hold of our body when we are in a low state of immunity. We need to put our attention on what we want, not what we don't want. Through creative visualization we need to begin seeing, feeling and thinking of ourselves in a state of vibrant health.

It is important to continue with sound medical treatment throughout the healing process whenever it is indicated, but don't allow anyone to instill a feeling of hopelessness in you.

Resentment, anger, fear, hatred and all of the other negative emotions we may feel toward the disease only compound the problem. Disease is a form of misqualified energy, and as we learned in Chapter 5, there is no way to destroy negative energy. All we can do is raise it back into a harmonious frequency of vibration, actually love it free. So instead of hating our disease, we need to work with it just like we do any other negative circumstance that is occurring in our life. We need to acknowledge that this is our own energy we misqualified at one time or another during our sojourn on Earth. We should then be grateful for the opportunity to transmute this energy back to its original perfection and ask for forgiveness for misqualifying this precious gift of life. Finally, we should fill the energy with the pink essence of pure love and literally love it free.

Recall the four activities:

1. *Acceptance*–Acknowledging it is our own misqualified energy.
2. *Gratitude*–For the opportunity to transmute the vibration of this misqualified energy back to its original perfection.
3. *Forgiveness*–For abusing our precious gift of life.
4. *Love*–Loving the misqualified energy back to a state of harmony.

These are catalysts in the healing process. After applying the four steps, we can accelerate the healing process by consciously accepting, through the efficacy of faith, our ability to use the full power of our mind to heal. Then reinforce this faith with positive affirmations, creative visualization, deliberately channeling healing energy into the body, controlled breathing exercises and the buoyant feeling of success. This process will be described later in this chapter.

I want to mention at this point that there comes a time in each of our lives when our learning experiences in the physical plane are completed. I think it's fairly safe to say no one is going to get off this planet "alive." In Richard Bach's wonderful book *Illusions,* he said there is a test to determine if one's work on Earth is finished. The test is, *if you're alive, it isn't.* The reason for mentioning this now is that often when we think of healing, we automatically think this means we will not have to leave the Earthplane. If our work here is completed, we are going to leave our physical body even if the healing is completed to perfection. The important thing to understand is that we can leave this physical realm in a state of perfect peace and harmony, instead of leaving through the process of an agonizing degenerative disease. So, regardless of whether or not it is time for us to make our transition into the fourth dimension, we still owe it to the precious life energy we have misqualified that is manifesting as a physical illness, to put forth every effort possible to restore it back to perfection–in other words, a perfect state of health.

There are some wonderful tools we can apply to accomplish this task. One of them is deep breathing. We are discovering that this "other energy" we have been discussing throughout this book can be drawn into the body and intensified with rhythmic breathing. In China this energy is called "Chi." In India it is called "Prana," and in the Bible it is called the "Holy Breath." When we consciously breathe this electronic Light Substance into our body, we can revitalize and rejuvenate every cell.

The more we practice rhythmic deep breathing, the sooner we will come to the realization that to breathe means to live, and by breathing properly we can help correct the negative conditions that are manifesting in our physical body. By learning to breathe evenly and directing the breath into our diseased cells, we can raise the vibratory action of our body. In so doing, each cell is cleansed, clearing away the effluvia which we have allowed to form. The majority of people have become so heavy with this self-created negative vibration of energy that they feel sluggish and tired most of the time. The following breathing exercises will improve our physical, etheric, mental, and emotional bodies, and by persevering, we will soon realize that we feel lighter in our physical body, free and unhindered in our thinking. We will experience a more joyous outlook on life, and, emotionally, we will be calmer, more serene in dealing with the situations that arise in our daily lives.

It is a good idea for us to set aside a time each day for these breathing exercises; they should be done at least twice a day. Both exercises will take a total of fifteen minutes at the most, and I promise you that the results you experience will be well worth your time.

Breathing Exercises

Before beginning any breathing exercises, it is important to empty the lungs of any stale air. To do this simply form your mouth in the shape of an "O" and exhale heavily while making an "ooh" sound.

1. For the first breathing exercise, stand erect, feet together, arms relaxed resting at your sides. As you begin to inhale slowly, tense the arms and raise them out from your sides and up over your head. This is done to a count of five. Then, hold your arms straight up over your head. As you hold the breath for the count of five, visualize a great White Light pouring down from your higher self, filling every cell of your physical body. Then, slowly exhale to the count of five, as you lower your arms to your side. Finally, hold the breath out to the count of five and relax your arms.

   Relax, and then repeat the exercise seven times. On completion of the seven breaths, relax and affirm to yourself with *deep feeling:*

   "I GIVE THANKS FOR MY LIFE, FOR MY PHYSICAL BODY, THE MOST WONDERFUL INSTRUMENT IN THE UNIVERSE. I NOW COMMAND THAT EVERY CELL, ATOM, GLAND, MUSCLE, ORGAN AND FUNCTION OF MY BODY ACCEPT THE BLAZING LIGHT FROM MY HIGHER SELF THAT HEALS, THAT RAISES AND MAKES WHOLE THIS TEMPLE OF THE LIVING GOD, AND I AM MOST GRATEFUL FOR MY PURE WELL-BALANCED BODY."

2. In this second breathing exercise you are making a decree for youth. Nearly everyone is desirous of feeling young, to be able to move in a beautiful rhythmic manner, to walk gracefully, to glow from inner joy and happiness. This can be accomplished by practicing this breathing exercise. It is important that you be a shining example. How are you going to prove the natural laws of the Universe if you yourself are not "the Light that shines in the darkness?"

   To begin this exercise, visualize yourself doing something you have not done in years–running up a hill, dashing into the ocean, leaping with gay abandon. *Feel the free buoyancy of youth.* Then stand with your arms at your side and take a slow, deep breath to the count of four. Holding the breath, raise your arms up forward and over your head, reaching back as far as you can, moving your head back until your face is looking heavenward.

Continue to hold the breath as you bend forward as far as you can comfortably. Continue holding the breath as you straighten up and raise your arms up and back over your head again. Then exhale, slowly bringing your arms down to the starting position at your side. Relax, and then repeat the exercise three times. On completion of the third breath, relax and affirm to yourself with *deep feeling:*

"I AM FILLED WITH THE LIGHT THAT REVITALIZES EVERY PART OF MY BODY. I AM FILLED WITH THAT GLOWING, GLORIOUS, VIBRANT FEELING OF YOUTH. I AM ALIVE WITH THE MOTIVATING POWER OF ACTION. I AM YOUNG, YOUNG, YOUNG. I AM ETERNAL YOUTH!"

Persistance is the key to success and after doing these exercises faithfully twice a day for a month, you will notice obvious changes in your awareness, your consciousness and your overall sense of well-being, which will give you the incentive to continue to your full self-mastery.

After completing the breathing exercises, at least once a day, sit comfortably in a chair and deliberately draw healing energy through every cell and organ of your body, concentrating specifically on your individual needs. This is done through concentration and creative visualization. Through the power of your attention, this healing energy will be intensified through the cells of your body, and the vibratory action will be accelerated.

The color green in all of its hues carries the frequency and vibration of healing. Therefore, this is the color to work with for this visualization.

Healing Visualization

For this exercise sit comfortably in a chair with your spine as straight as possible and your arms and legs uncrossed. This allows you to be a clear channel for the healing energy without blocking the flow by closing off the circuits. If you would like, you may put on some beautiful, harmonious music to help you relax and be at peace.

To begin the exercise breathe in deeply, exhale, and completely relax. Feel all of the tension, doubt, or fear just drop away. This is a very special time just for you, and anything that you need to take care of will be waiting for you when you're through, so for the time being just set it aside. This is a special time for you to draw healing energy from the Universal Source of all Life through every electron of your four lower bodies to heal, restore, and rejuvenate these vehicles back into a perfect state of health. For a moment concentrate on the four-fold activity of acceptance, gratitude, forgiveness and love as it pertains to the health of your own individual being. Then breathe in deeply again, and, as you exhale, visualize coming down from above you a blazing ray of Emerald Green Light from the heart of the Universal Source of all Life. This is a pure ray of healing energy. It enters the top of your head, and you experience the scintillating Light Substance as it passes through each system of your body—healing, cleansing, purifying, and restoring each cell back to perfect health.

Through deep concentration, visualize this Emerald Green Light as it passes through your body system by system. It first begins to expand through the

1.   Brain Structure—removing all disease and raising your conscious awareness, increasing your ability to use the power of your mind.
2.   Eyes—restoring them to perfect sight, allowing you to recognize perfection in all life.

3. Ears–restoring them to perfect hearing and sound, allowing you to hear the "still small voice within" of your higher self, as well as the music of the spheres.
4. Nose–restoring perfect smell and breathing.
5. Sinuses–removing all disease.
6. Mouth, teeth, gums, tongue and lips–restoring your health and allowing perfect speech with every word you speak, so every word will be a blessing to all life.
7. Entire head structure–restoring perfect balance.
8. Apastate Control Center at base of skull–restoring perfect eating habits.
9. Spinal Column and Spinal Cord–restoring perfect alignment and distribution of electronic energy.
10. Nervous System–restoring perfect health and calm.
11. Lymphatic System: Lymph nodes and lymphatic fluid–restoring perfect health.
12. Endocrine System–concentrated healing through pituitary and pineal glands, as well as thyroid, thymus, pancreas, spleen, adrenal, gonads, and all other glands associated with this ductless system of glands.
13. Chakras–restoring perfect balance and harmony to this energy system.
14. Respiratory System: Nasal passage, larnyx, trachea, bronchial tubes, lungs–restoring perfect health by removing all pollution or disease, enabling you to absorb the maximum prana on The Holy Breath.
15. Circulatory System: Heart, muscle, chambers, valves, veins, arteries, capillaries, red and white blood cells, bone marrow–restoring perfect health, balance and harmony.
16. Digestive System: Esophagus, stomach, liver, gallbladder, small intestines, ileocecal valve, large intestines, appendix, colon, kidneys, bladder, and all systems of elimination–restoring perfect health, cleansing and balancing this system.
17. Reproductive System: Male and female organs–restor-

ing perfect health, and for those lifestreams that will be bringing in the children of the New Age, creating clear chalices so that all of these beautiful incoming children will have perfect vehicles through which to function in the physical world of form.

18. Skeletal System: Bones, joints, tendons, ligaments, cartilage and all connective tissue–restoring perfect health, removing every trace of degeneration and disease.

19. Muscular System–restoring it to strong youthful form, removing every trace of degeneration and disease.

20. Fat System–removing all unnecessary cells, restoring this system to firm efficient flesh.

21. Skin, Hair, Nails–removing every line, blemish or sign of aging or degeneration and restoring these cells to radiantly beautiful, youthful form.

22. Etheric Body–removing all unpleasant memories, all inharmonious records or vibrations, revivifying all constructive thoughtforms, activities and memories that will assist you in reaching your highest potential.

23. Mental Body–removing all destructive thought processes, establishing new constructive thoughtforms.

24. Emotional Body–removing all discordant, inharmonious feelings and emotions and restoring your ability to continually radiate forth feelings of love, peace, comfort, happiness, joy, harmony, and general well-being.

Now, as this healing Emerald Green Light is pulsating in, through, and around every electron of your four lower bodies, you have the ability to project it forth to bless your friends and loved ones, as well as all life on this sweet Earth.

Visualize standing before you your friends and loved ones to whom you would like to render specific healing. Through the power of your thoughts, their higher selves or super conscious minds will absorb this healing energy and channel it through their four lower bodies, no matter where they are on this entire planet. Project forth now from your heart center a mighty laser beam of emerald green healing energy, and visualize it entering their heart centers. As it enters their hearts, it begins to expand as a tremendous starburst out through their four lower bodies, filling them with healing light, cleansing, purifying, restoring, and healing every electron back to its perfect frequency of vibration.

You now have the ability to expand this healing energy to any place on the planet you feel needs to be healed. This should be your individual choice, but to accelerate the manifestation of world peace, let's blaze this healing light in, through, and around every single person associated in any way, shape or form with the governments of this planet, healing, aligning, and balancing their physical, etheric, mental, and emotional bodies, so their higher selves can get through to their conscious minds and bring them illumination, wisdom, and truth, quickly raising their awareness to the oneness of all life, the Universal Family of Humanity.

As this healing light is blazing through all the governments on this planet, you have the opportunity to join forces with other light workers and form a mighty transformer into the physical realm to create a forcefield to magnetize the pure essence of Eternal Peace from the heart of the Universal Source of all Life into physical manifestation. And add the gift of your precious life energy to the following forcefield for world peace.

Forcefield for World Peace

Visualize pulsating in the atmosphere the luminous planet Earth, giving off a soft pink glow of pure Love. Encircling the planet are the hands of all nations, joined together in a forcefield of Unity. Above this luminous globe is a brilliant Dove of Peace sending forth the Golden Rays of Peace Eternal into all life on the planet. From the Divine Momentum within the center of the Earth the healing power of Living, Loving Truth pierces outward into the receptive consciousness of All Life. The purified keynote of the planet Earth resounds throughout the rejoicing Universe.

As you hold this thoughtform in your consciousness, magnetize it into the physical realm by affirming to yourself seven
times: "I Am" the Restoration of the Family of Humanity
through the Abiding Presence of Love, Peace and
Truth... The Oneness of all Life.

The more we activate this forcefield through the power of
our attention, the more quickly we will see world peace become a reality. We have the ability to join forces with our
friends, loved ones, neighbors, co-workers, groups, activities, associates, and on and on, to increase our effectiveness in magnetizing peace from the octaves of perfection into
the physical realm. When a seemingly miraculous healing has
occurred, what actually took place was that the vibratory rate
of the cells of the person's body was accelerated to a harmonious frequency, and the disease was cast off. This can occur
instantly, or it may be a gradual acceleration, depending on
the person's effectiveness in channeling healing energy. But,
the important thing to remember is that no sincere effort is
ever lost. Each time we draw healing energy, whether it is to
heal ourselves, our loved ones, or the planet itself, we are increasing the Light of the World and consequently raising the
vibratory rate of all life on the planet.

Each and every person on this planet can be an effective
channel to increase the Light and Perfection for all life evolving here and truly transform this Blessed Earth into Freedom's
Holy Star.

Affirmation of Healing

"I Am" expanding the Light within my heart center throughout my physical body.

I COMMAND all of the vibrating impulses in my physical,
etheric, mental and emotional bodies, which are of a destructive nature to CEASE RIGHT NOW! and FOREVER!...and be
replaced by the Healing Light from the Universal Source. This
Light is rebuilding every cell and organ of my bodies into Per-

fect Health and Manifestations of HARMONY!

What I ask for myself, I ask also for my loved ones and all mankind. "I Am" sending this Healing Energy to all Hospitals, Nursing Homes, Mental Institutions, and Institutions of Healing throughout the world.

I accept that this healing activity has been completed with Full Power for "I Am" the Power of Healing in Action *NOW!*

SO BE IT!

8

The Mysterious Chakras

Chakra is a Sanskrit word that means "wheel". It is used to describe the various vortices of energy that are located in our four lower bodies. The chakras serve the purpose of distributing the electronic light from the Universal Source throughout our bodies. Through my studies I have found that these energy centers are sometimes considered mysterious and often misunderstood. It is important to demystify the chakras so that we can learn how to use them as a practical tool in our self-development.

In order for us to become the masters of our lives we need to know as much as possible about the intricate forces that affect every aspect of our well-being. Through self-awareness, as is evident in that age-old adage *"Man know thyself,"* we can learn to work with the natural laws that influence every circumstance of our being and actually change the course of our lives. We can take command of our present life situations and steer any destructive patterns or behaviors back to the path of harmony and happiness.

The chakras are a little-known and yet vitally important part of the victory of self-mastery. In the ancient oriental sciences of yoga and acupuncture the chakras have always been an important factor in healing and spiritual enlightenment, but in the western world we, for the most part, have discounted

their existence. Until recently, science couldn't seem to logically trace the invisible pathways through which the electrical
energy passes in the physical body; so, the practice of
acupuncture didn't seem to be valid.

In the past few years, research into the supposedly non-
existent energy fields in and around the physical body has
been greatly accelerated, and, through the advancement of
modern technology, the scientific world is no longer denying
the existence of the energy centers or chakras. For the scientific world, this is a new discovery. Our knowledge of the
seven major chakra centers and the lesser chakras that function in the body, and what their full development will mean
to the evolution of mankind, is still in the embryonic stage.

I would like to share with you what I have concluded
through much research and observation. The activity of these
vortices of energy in the body, the chakras, seems to be two-
fold. They function on a physical as well as a spiritual level,
both material and ethereal, or third dimensional and fourth
dimensional. It has been observed that, if there are imbalances
or malfunctions on a physical level in any one of the seven
major chakras or the lesser chakras, the result will be a blockage of energy to the cells or organs of the body that are fed
through the acupuncture meridian from that chakra, which
will result in the disintegration of that cell or organ and ultimately allow disease to take hold.

The science of kinesiology, blended with the application
of acupuncture, is discovering a means of muscle testing
to locate blockages in the energy fields and reverse the degenerative process by restoring the flow of energy to the
meridian affecting the specific cell or organ. By exploring the
functions of the seven major chakras, we can discover what
their unfoldment will mean in our efforts to reach our highest
potential.

The chakra centers are vortices of energy that form a system
through which energy flows from one of our four lower
bodies to another. Anyone who possesses a slight degree of

etheric vision may easily see the chakra centers pulsating in the etheric body. The size, radiance, power, and activity of the chakras in each individual are determined by many factors. On the spiritual or fourth dimensional level, as each person matures spiritually, develops mastery and self-control, and learns to channel energy constructively, their chakra centers begin to grow, unfold, develop, spin, and emit more light. When the chakras are undeveloped on the spiritual level, they are about two inches in diameter and appear as small circles. The light emanating from them is weak and rather dim. The rotation of the chakra is slow, and it appears almost stationary or dormant. As each chakra begins to develop and unfold through the conscious self-mastery of the individual, it begins to awaken and emit more light as it opens. The spiritually awakened or opened chakra appears as a radiant, spinning, convex vortex of energy emanating brilliant light, color, and texture, and it is several inches in diameter.

At the present time this spiritual development of the chakras is just beginning to unfold in the large majority of people. In fact, from outer appearances, the spiritual development appears to be almost dormant in most people.

On the physical or third dimensional level the development of the chakras is quite different, and this seems to be where all of the confusion lies. Most of the chakra books I have read are dealing with the development of the chakras on a physical level and confusing it with spiritual growth. My goal in this chapter is to try and present the two functioning levels of the chakras clearly enough so that we can experience our individual growth, both on a physical as well as spiritual level, and effectively use our chakras as a tool to greater awareness.

To begin with, let's look at the development and function of the seven major chakras on a physical level. The color, tone, and quality of the energy being emitted from the chakra centers on the physical level is very different from the color, tone, and quality being emitted on the spiritual level. It is important, and even necessary, for us to recognize this distinction and learn to perceive the difference in these two energy fields. The more we tune in to these chakras and begin consciously working with them, the more sensitive we will become, and before long we will be able to easily discern the physical vibration from the spiritual vibration.

All of our chakras function actively on the physical level as long as we have a physical body. These chakras are the transformers that receive the electronic Light Substance from the Universal Source and then transmit it to the rest of our four lower bodies. This activity is continually ongoing as long as we are in a physical body and, therefore, is occurring in every single person on the planet regardless of the individual's spiritual development. The important point for us to understand is that an *active* chakra does not mean a spiritually awakened or developed chakra. It merely means that the chakra is performing its proper function on the physical level. The colors that emanate from the seven major chakras on the physical level reflect the base octave of color which is known as the pigment octave. This octave of color manifests as form and is the densest color and the easiest to see. Therefore, it is the physical pigment octave that is usually described in chakra books.

On the physical level the base pigment octave that emanates from the Root Chakra at the base of the spine is red, the Central Chakra located in the mid-abdomen is orange, the Solar Plexus Chakra located at the navel is yellow, the Heart Chakra is green, the Throat Chakra is blue, the Third Eye Chakra located between the brows is indigo and the Crown Chakra at the top of the head is violet.

The seven major chakras are anchored in the physical body along the spine. There is, actually, what I would call an etheric stem physically anchored in the spine which extends out to the wheel of the chakra floating on the surface of the etheric body. This chakra system is the means by which all of our four lower bodies are brought into relation with each other. These vortices of energy govern the endocrine system which, in turn, controls the seven major areas of the physical body and is responsible for the correct functioning of the entire organism producing both physiological and psychological effects. The seven chakra centers are not *in* the physical body, but rather *float* on the surface of the etheric body and are anchored in the physical body only through the etheric stem. They are close to the same region where the seven major glands of the endocrine system are located, and each chakra provides the power and life force of the corresponding gland which is, in fact, its externalization.

The chakras and their physical counterparts are as follows:

Crown Chakra . . . . Pituitary Gland
Third Eye Chakra . . . . Pineal Gland
Throat Chakra . . . . Thyroid Gland
Heart Chakra . . . . Thymus Gland
Solar Plexus Chakra . . . . Pancreas
Central Chakra . . . . Adrenal Gland
Root Chakra . . . . The Gonads

The electronic Light Substance from the Universal Source enters the top of our head in a continual stream of billions and billions of electrons.

As this energy enters the top of our head, it begins to pass back and forth through the spinal cord on specific pathways down to the Root Chakra at the base of the spine. These pathways are divided into two polarities. One is the feminine aspect of this force and is called the Ida. The other is the masculine aspect of this force and is called the Pingala. Once this energy reaches the Root Chakra at the base of the spine, it begins its ascent back up the spine, and, as it does, it transmits the energy through the seven major chakras, which in turn send the energy forth into the various cells of our body via the electrical meridians. This is the means through which this gift of life sustains our existence in the physical realm.

As this energy is being transmitted through the chakras to the various parts of the body, the vortices themselves appear very active, and, depending on how healthy or vital we are, the radiation will be stronger or weaker, and the colors will be, proportionally, more or less vivid. A strong vibration and vivid clear color at the physical level of vibration is often interpreted to mean spiritual development, when, in fact, all it means is a healthy body. As we develop our ability to tune in to this frequency of vibration, we will be able to tell a great deal about our health and general well-being and use this information as a tool to improve the quality of our life.

Muddy distorted colors may indicate a problem in the transmitting of energy. By tracing the meridians out to the various points through acupuncture and kinesiological techniques, we can usually find the blockage and restore the flow of energy. Distorted colors can also indicate a problem at the etheric, mental, or emotional level that is affecting the physical body. By passing our hands over these centers, we will eventually be able to feel the various frequencies of vibration and detect malfunctions or discordant vibrations. Then we will, at least, have an idea of where the problem is, and we can begin taking steps to correct it.

I know that when you first begin thinking of the possibility of seeing etheric colors or feeling vibrations of energy, it seems very mystical and supernatural, but in actuality, it is a perfectly natural part of growth and development. There are many people at the present time who are experiencing what seems to be intuitive, or clairvoyant, or extra-sensory types of phenomena in their lives. This is occurring because it is time in our evolution for all humanity to move into a higher octave of awareness, and there are always some people who will begin to develop that awareness before others. We don't all step into a higher consciousness at the same moment, but we can accelerate that elevation of conscious awareness by deliberately tuning in to the forces of energy around us and striving, through self-discipline, to become the masters of our lives. Initially, it is not important for you to see the colors or feel the vibrations, but I want you to be aware that it is a natural result of your self-mastery so you will be receptive to it when it begins to occur in your life.

If you understand the function and effects of your chakras on a physical level, it will help you to keep your four lower bodies operating at a frequency of perfect health and help you to keep these vehicles aligned and balanced. But, if you understand the function and effects of your chakras on a spiritual level, you can truly transform your life. So, let's now begin exploring the much misunderstood spiritual unfoldment of this chakra system.

Within the center of the physical chakra is a vortex of energy that is vibrating at a much higher frequency and appears as a pulsating stamen within the chakra flower. This is known as the spiritual chakra. In the average person this chakra is *closed* and looks much like the bud of a flower. The light being emitted from this center is usually so weak that the base octave of pigment color from the physical chakra overpowers it, and often the physical color is all that can be seen.

The purpose of our spiritual chakras is to provide avenues into the physical realm through which we can draw the perfect qualities of the octaves of Light and channel them into physical manifestation, while at the same time attaining personal self-mastery and enlightenment. That may sound like a heavy statement, but I am going to discuss it in detail so that you can use this tool effectively as you strive towards your victorious accomplishment of self-mastery.

Because of all of the confusing information available about chakras, I think it is a good idea to set aside any preconceived notions for the time being and read the following information with an open, objective mind.

On a spiritual level, under the direction of our higher self or super-conscious mind, the electronic Light Substance from the Universal Source enters the top of our heads and passes back and forth through the spinal cord along the same Ida and Pingala pathways as it does on the physical level down to the Root Chakra, but on its ascent a very different activity takes place. On the return current, the spiritual electronic Light

Substance ascends directly up the center of the spine, and according to our development, this energy passes through the spiritual chakra and radiates into the world to form a specific virtue, quality, color, and tone.

Our higher selves know exactly how much pressure to apply to each chakra according to our individual growth, and the more self-mastery we have attained, the greater activity of Light we can release into the physical plane. As this Light is pressed through our spiritual chakra in exact proportion to our spiritual development, the chakra slowly *opens* and our conscious awareness is raised, and our ability to release more Light is increased.

When we evolve to the point of having all of our spiritual chakras opened, we will reach what is known as true enlightenment–in reality, our highest potential.

The medical symbol of the caduceus that had its inception with the founding of medicine in ancient Greece is in actuality a representation of our gift of life. The two serpents interweaving back and forth up the staff represent the Ida and Pingala energy. The staff up the middle of the symbol is symbolic of the rising spiritual energy. The winged globe at the top of the staff symbolizes spiritual freedom and enlightenment. In Eastern Philosophy this activity of raising the spiritual energy and opening the spiritual chakras is called the Kundalini, or raising the spiritual fire.

This is an activity that occurs *naturally* in every person on this planet as one develops through self-mastery. This is not something that we must believe in. It is another aspect of natural law. The advantage of knowing about it is that there are things we can do to co-operate with this natural unfoldment that will enable us to be more effective forces of Light on this planet.

It is important we understand that this opening of our spiritual chakras occurs *naturally as we grow spiritually.* I have read books and encountered groups that are operating under the erroneous and extremely dangerous notion that somehow we can speed up our enlightenment by forcing the chakras open through various exercises such as extreme fasting, or an activity called the Breath of Fire, or other unnatural means. I cannot stress emphatically enough that *there are no short cuts for spiritual growth*.

Forcing the chakras open before we have developed spiritually or attained self-mastery, or before they have been purified and balanced, can cause all kinds of problems and bring chaos and destruction into our lives, even irreversible insanity. Forcing the chakras open does not raise us into a higher consciousness; it just forces us to emit more energy at whatever level of consciousness we are currently functioning. The purpose of the spiritual chakras is to release constructive qualities into the physical realm, but, unfortunately, there is an opposite polarity to each virtue. So, if we haven't attained self-mastery, and we are still misqualifying energy through our thoughts, words, and deeds, forcing the chakras open allows more energy to pass through us. Consequently, we can misqualify greater amounts of energy. This, in turn, means greater amounts of negativity returning to us, and it can cause our ultimate downfall.

Our higher selves are anxiously awaiting our growth and development, and the *moment* we can constructively release more energy, our higher selves seize the opportunity and apply greater pressure to open the spiritual chakra a slight degree. This is an automatic occurrence; our responsibility is not to worry about opening the chakras but, rather, to gain control of our thoughts, words, and deeds.

So, if this process of opening the spiritual chakras occurs naturally as we attain self-mastery, how can we effect changes in our lives through an awareness of these chakras?

The answer to that question is that the natural laws of this universe are based on logic and order, and every particle of life has a purpose and reason for being and interrelates to every other particle of life. In this instance, the chakras are no exception. There are seven specific energy fields that interpenetrate the planet Earth. As the pure white Light comes forth from the Universal Source of all Life and reaches the atmosphere of Earth, it bends as it encircles the planet, giving the same effect as sending light through a prism. This white Light is then divided into seven colors, the same as the spectrum of a rainbow, and these seven bands of color form spheres around the Earth. Each of these seven spheres has its own specific frequency of vibration, quality, tone, virtue, fragrance, and color.

These spheres are often referred to in ancient philosophy as the Seven Rays, or the "Seven Spirits Before the Throne," or the "Seven Lords of Flame." For our purposes here, I'll call them the Seven Rays. Each one of these rays corresponds to one of our seven major spiritual chakras, and the original purpose of these spiritual chakras was to channel the virtue, quality, fragrance, color, and tone of the respective ray into the physical world of form.

As mankind began using life energy for things other than *good*, our higher selves began closing off the energy flowing from the Seven Rays through the chakras as a merciful activity so we would not totally destroy ourselves with our own miscreations. Gradually, our spiritual chakras became almost dormant. Now, as we are striving toward a higher consciousness, self-mastery, and awareness, our higher selves are gradually opening these vortices of energy again so we can once more be constructive channels for the qualities of this perfect Light substance into the world of form.

What we must understand is that for something to manifest in the physical realm, it must be drawn through a physical body. That is natural law. Everything we could possibly need or want already exists in the unformed Light substance of the fourth dimension, but to draw it into a physical manifestation, we must consciously magnetize it through our thoughts, feelings, and attention. Throughout history, philosophers, sages, and seers have been foretelling of an eventual *Heaven on Earth*. That perfection is already pulsating in every detail in the etheric realms, but in order for us to bring it into a physical reality on Earth, we must magnetize that perfection through our four lower bodies into the physical realm.

This can be done through our conscious efforts by deliberately drawing the perfect qualities of the Seven Rays through our seven major chakras. The end result of this activity is two-fold. By channeling more Light into the planet, we accelerate our own growth, bringing us closer to our highest potential. We also assist in transforming the planet into a virtual "Heaven on Earth." As this constructive energy from the Seven Rays passes through our chakras into the world of form, it purifies, aligns and balances our chakras, enabling them to be both radiating and magnetizing centers of constructive, positive energy. Pulsating through the spiritual chakras is the highest vibration of color from the Octaves of Light. The Light Octave of color is very different from the base octave of pigment.

I will go over each chakra and the corresponding ray so you will understand these centers and be able to use this activity of channeling light as an effective tool. Let's begin with the Root Chakra located in the area of the base of the spine (see Figure 2, p. 119). As we go over these chakra centers, I am going to discuss the positive qualities that should be emanating from each vortex, as well as the opposite negative polarity that is at the present time emanating, at least on occasion, in the majority of people. At the end of this chapter, I am going to give an exercise to consciously draw purifying energy through each chakra so we can cleanse, align, and balance these vortices of energy and quickly change the activity of each one from negative to positive.

The Root Chakra is located at the base of the spine and corresponds to the fourth sphere of color around the planet or the Fourth Ray, which is white and vibrates with the qualities of purity, perfection, and restoration. In the spiritually developed person, this chakra appears as a convex-spinning vortex of blazing white light and continually radiates out the

qualities of purity, perfection, and restoration. In the undeveloped person, the chakra is almost stationary and dormant.
In the negative or destructive person, this chakra is concave
and sometimes even rotates in the opposite direction; instead
of radiating out the positive quality of purity, it actually draws
in the opposite polarity which is lust or sexual imbalance. This
can have different degrees of effect on sexual activity from
mild promiscuity to violent sex crimes. By observing what is
going on in the world today, with the so-called sexual revolution and increase in sexual crimes, we can see that there is a
great deal of imbalance in the Root Chakra.

The next chakra, located in the area of the mid-abdomen
below the navel, is called the Central Chakra. This chakra corresponds to the Seventh Ray, which is violet and vibrates with
the qualities of mercy, compassion, forgiveness, transmutation, invocation, and freedom. In the developed person, it is
a convex-spinning vortex of violet light radiating forth the
above virtues. In the undeveloped person, it remains dormant. In the negative person, it draws in the opposite polarity
which manifests as anger, hatred, or even mild dislike. By observing the negative polarities of these energy fields, we can
see that probably all of us are out of balance to some degree in
one or more of the chakras, at least on occasion.

The next chakra is located in the area of the navel and is
known as the Solar Plexus Chakra. This center corresponds to
the Sixth Ray and is ruby gold, which includes the entire spectrum of gold and ruby as well as any combination of the two
colors, from pale peach to deep orange. This ray vibrates with
the qualities of peace, healing, and ministration in the developed person. In the undeveloped person, it is dormant. In
the negative person, the opposite polarity of this ray manifests as fear, gluttony, greed, or excesses of any kind. You
have probably experienced twinges of fear and felt that grip-
ping in your solar plexus, or had "butterflies" in your
stomach, or that "gut feeling" at one time or another. That
sensation comes from the Solar Plexus Chakra.

The three lower chakras we have just covered are humanity's most active and volatile chakras at the present time. They are more subject to contamination and to drawing in negative energy than the other chakras.

The next center is the Heart Chakra, and it corresponds to the Third Ray, which is pink. This ray vibrates with the frequency of pure love; the Heart Chakra joins and balances the three lower chakras and the three higher chakras. In the developed person, this is a powerful forcefield of Divine Love. In the undeveloped person, it's dormant. The opposite polarity of the Third Ray manifests in the negative person as laziness, lethargy, boredom, and depression.

The next chakra is located in the area of the throat and corresponds to the First Ray, which is sapphire blue. The Throat Chakra is our power center and vibrates with the frequency of God's Will, illumined faith, power and protection in the developed individual. The imbalances of this chakra, or the opposite polarities of the First Ray, manifest in a negative person as envy, personal power, jealousy, self-righteousness, and arrogance.

The next center is the Third Eye Chakra and is located in the area between the brows. This chakra corresponds to the Fifth Ray, which is emerald green and vibrates with the qualities of truth, healing, concentration, consecration, and inner vision in the developed person. The opposite polarities of this ray manifest as selfish pride, doubt, intellectual arrogance, and conceit in the negative person.

The last of the seven major chakras is located in the area of the top of the head and is called the Crown Chakra. As this chakra unfolds and opens, it appears as a many-pointed star and is often referred to as the thousand-petal lotus blossom. This center corresponds to the Second Ray, which is sunshine yellow and vibrates with the qualities of God Illumination, wisdom, understanding, and enlightenment in the developed person. This is our most spiritual center. At the present stage of evolution, our higher selves are protecting this chakra from contamination; so, fortunately, if this chakra is not developing positively, it remains dormant and no negative polarity is manifesting through it.

In order to cleanse, align and balance these seven major chakras, we need to learn how to consciously blaze the light of the corresponding ray through each center. By doing this, we raise the vibration of the chakra to a higher frequency and prevent the negative polarity from manifesting in our thoughts, feelings, emotions, or actions. This is a tremendous assistance to us as we are striving to take charge of our lives and eliminate our self-defeating behavior. If any one of our chakras is out of balance and magnetizing the negative polarities mentioned into our mental and emotional bodies, it greatly interferes with our efforts to gain control of our thoughts and feelings.

Again, I'll mention that we are actually residing in a sea of negativity because of the tremendous amount of negativity being emitted from people all over the world. If our mid-Chakra is out of balance, for example, and we are magnetizing the opposite polarity (anger, hatred, or even mild dislike) into our lives, because of the overwhelming amount of hatred reverberating through the atmosphere, we can be bombarded with so much of this destructive energy that we will reflect anger and hatred in every aspect of our lives, no matter how hard we try through sheer will power to control it. This can be true of any one or or all of the negative polarities, so it is vital that we strive to cleanse, balance, and align all our chakras. This can be accomplished through creative visualization and deliberately invoking our higher selves to blaze the Light of the Seven Rays through each respective chakra.

If you are becoming aware of the chakras for the first time, they may seem very complicated and confusing to you. It's not important that you fully understand every detail of the function of these energy centers. Actually, no one fully understands them yet. The only thing that is important for you to understand right now is that, if you ask your higher self to increase the God qualities of the Seven Rays through your seven major chakras and visualize that pure Light pouring through each corresponding chakra, as I will describe in the following exercise, you will greatly improve the quality of your life and begin taking quantum leaps towards your highest potential.

As you begin this exercise, you should sit comfortably in a chair with your arms and legs uncrossed and your spine as straight as possible. Beautiful harmonious music always assists in raising your vibrations, so music may be playing softly in the background. You should expel all of the stale air from your lungs and then breathe in deeply and completely relax.

One of the qualities of the Seventh Ray is transmutation. That means the frequency of the violet energy from the Seventh Ray changes the vibration of discordant or impure energy back to its original perfection. This quality will greatly accelerate the process of purifying your chakras. So, to begin your visualization, first purify the chakras with the energy of the Seventh Ray as follows:

Chakra Cleansing and Balancing Exercise

As you completely relax, close your eyes and visualize coming down from above you a blazing Violet Light, the color of crystalline amethyst. This scintillating Light Substance enters the top of your head and descends down your spine into the Root Chakra. As it enters this vortex of energy, it begins to expand as a powerful starburst filling the Root Chakra with violet transmuting energy. This Violet Light blazes in, through, and around every electron of this chakra, cleansing, purifying and balancing this center, removing all discordant frequencies of vibration and transforming this chakra back to its original perfection.

The Violet Transmuting Light now ascends into the Central Chakra, performing the exact same service and transforming this vortex of energy into its perfect function. It then rises into the Solar Plexus Chakra, transmuting this center into its perfect function. Then this Violet Light ascends into the Heart Chakra, then the Throat Chakra, then the Third Eye Chakra, and finally the Crown Chakra, performing its perfect activity of transmutation every step of the way until each of the seven major chakras is cleansed, aligned, balanced, and purified to the maximum that natural law will allow according to each individual need.

After this activity has been completed, your chakras are now ready to blaze the perfect qualities of the Seven Rays into your individual world and then out to the rest of the planet.

To begin this activity, visualize a blazing ray of White Light from the Fourth Sphere coming down from above and entering the top of your head. The pure White Light descends into the Root Chakra at the base of the spine and, through this purified center, begins radiating the energy and vibration of the Fourth Ray into your life. This spiritual chakra center is transformed into a blazing white diamond as the virtues of purity, perfection and restoration begin filling every aspect of your life.

Next, visualize a blazing ray of Violet Light from the Seventh Sphere coming down from above and entering the top of your head. The pure Violet Light descends into the Mid-Chakra located in the area of your abdomen and begins radiating out through this purified center the qualities of the Seventh Ray: transmutation, invocation, mercy, compassion, forgiveness, and freedom. These virtues begin filling your world and permeating every aspect of your life. As this activity is taking place, this spiritual chakra is transformed into a blazing amethyst.

Next, visualize a blazing ray of Golden Light with a radiance of Ruby from the Sixth Sphere coming down from above and entering the top of your head as it descends into the Solar Plexus Chakra in the area of the navel. The Ruby Gold Light begins radiating out through this purified center the qualities of the Sixth Ray: peace, healing, and ministration. These virtues begin filling your world and permeating every aspect of your life. As this activity is taking place, this spiritual chakra is transformed into a blazing topaz.

Next, visualize a blazing ray of Pink Light from the Third Sphere coming from above and entering the top of your head as it descends into your Heart Chakra. The pure Pink Light begins radiating out through this purified center the qualities of the Third Ray, pure divine love. This virtue begins filling your world and permeating every aspect of your life. As this activity is taking place, this spiritual chakra is transformed into a flaming pink crystal heart of divine love.

Next, visualize a blazing ray of Sapphire Blue Light from the First Sphere coming down from above and entering the top of your head as it descends into the Throat Chakra. The Sapphire Blue Light begins radiating out through this purified center the qualities of the First Ray: God's Will, illumined faith, power and protection. These virtues begin filling your world and permeating every aspect of your life. As this activity is taking place, this spiritual chakra is transformed into a blazing sapphire.

Next, visualize a blazing ray of Emeral Green Light from the Fifth Sphere coming down from above and entering the top of your head as it descends into the Third Eye Chakra. The Emerald Green Light begins radiating out through this purified center the qualities of the Fifth Ray: truth, healing, concentration, consecration, and inner vision. These virtues begin filling your world and permeating every aspect of your life. As this activity is taking place, this spiritual chakra is transformed into a blazing emerald.

Next, visualize a blazing ray of Sunshine Yellow Light from the Second Sphere coming down from above and entering the top of your head as it descends into the Crown Chakra. The Sunshine Yellow Light begins radiating out through this purified center the qualities of the Second Ray: God Illumination, wisdom, understanding, and enlightenment. These virtues begin filling your world and permeating every aspect of your life. As this activity is taking place, this spiritual chakra is transformed into a blazing sun, a yellow diamond.

These etheric jewels that have been formed in your chakra centers through the power of this Light are, in actuality, crystallized Sacred Fire, and they form a powerful magnet to magnetize the God qualities of the Seven Rays into your life.

On completion of this exercise, invoke your higher self to continue to blaze the perfect qualities of the Seven Rays through your purified, aligned, and balanced spiritual chakras until each center is out-picturing its original perfection and function.

You must understand and know that you have the ability to intensify this activity through you at any time by the process of invocation and visualization; simply ask the Universal Source of all Life to project forth this perfect Light and then visualize it as it pours through each chakra center.

FIGURE 2

The New Age Study of Humanity's Purpose

Chakra	Ray	Area	Gland	Positive Traits	Negative Traits
1. Crown	2nd Ray Sunshine Yellow	Crown of head	Pituitary	God Illumination, Wisdom, Understanding, Enlightenment	None
2. Third Eye	5th Ray Emerald Green	Between Eyebrows	Pineal	Truth, Healing, Inner Vision, Concentration, Consecration	Selfish Pride, Doubt, Intellectual Arrogance, Conceit
3. Throat	1st Ray Sapphire Blue	Throat	Thyroid	God's Will, Power, Illumined Faith, Protection	Envy, Jealousy, Personal Power, Self-Righteousness, Arrogance
4. Heart	3rd Ray Pink	Heart	Thymus	Divine Love	Lethargy, Laziness, Boredom, Depression
5. Solar Plexus	6th Ray Ruby-Gold	Navel	Pancreas	Peace, Healing, Ministration	Greed, Gluttony, Fear
6. Central	7th Ray Violet	Spleen	Adrenal	Transmutation, Forgiveness, Freedom, Invocation, Mercy, Compassion	Anger, Hate, Dislike
7. Root	4th Ray White	Base of Spine	Gonads	Purity, Perfection, Restoration	Lust, Sexual Imbalance

9

The Use of Color to Help You Reach Your Highest Potential

This universe is filled with the vibrant essence of color, and we are discovering that color can be used for reasons far more significant than just esthetic beauty. Color is actually Light vibrating at various frequencies and is produced as pure white light from the Universal Source passes through the ethers and bends around the planet. Light travels at the rate of 186,000 miles per second and it produces waves varying from three one-hundred-thousandths of an inch in the case of infrared light to half that for ultraviolet light. When light vibrates at a rate of less than thirty impulses per second, it is generally invisible to our physical eye.

In recent years, there has been a great deal of research into the effect of color on the mental, emotional, and physical well-being of humans. Color is gradually being introduced into the medical world for its therapeutic value. It is also being used in places of employment, hospitals, mental institutions, prisons, schools, and home environments because of the effect it has on the emotions and mental attitudes of the people in those locations.

The Pittsburg Plate Glass Company of Tampa, Florida, issued a booklet on *Color Dynamics for the House*. The following is a quote from the article entitled "Utilize the Energy of Color":

> Laboratory tests and practical experience prove that there is Energy in Color which affects your health, comfort, happiness, and safety. By using the Energy in Color, you can paint yourself a home not only lovely to look at but also lovely to live in.
>
> When our color engineers started their study of the use of color in industry, educational institutions, office buildings, stores and homes, they were determined to explore the physiological and psychological reactions and benefits that occur in these various fields of operation.
>
> Their conclusions were that these things are due to the Energy in Color. Color, in the form of light, is part of the electro-magnetic spectrum. Light is one of its many octaves; others are cosmic rays, gamma rays, x-rays, ultraviolet rays, infra-red rays, radio and television rays – all possessing energy, yes, all, including light, possessing energy. Science has established these facts:
>
> 1. All electro-magnetic waves are identical except in wave length and frequency.
>
> 2. All types of radiant energy travel at the same rate of speed – 186,000 miles per second, and this, divided by the wave length of each, establishes its frequency.
>
> 3. Each color has a definite wave length – from 1/16 to 1/32 millionth of an inch – and therefore varies in frequency and impact force.
>
> 4. The value of each hue is controlled by its amplitude, light values having greater amplitude than dark values.
>
> 5. The waves of the electro-magnetic spectrum serve an almost limitless number of uses – radio, television, infra-red photography, ultraviolet lamps, fluorescent lights and x-ray machines.
>
> Since the many types of rays in the electro-magnetic spectrum possess great energy and perform definite

functions, it is a fact that light rays, which are part of this spectrum, possess usable energy.

Variation in the number of impacts upon the eye affects muscular, mental and nervous activity. For example, tests show that under ordinary light, muscular activity is twenty-three empirical units. It advances slightly under blue light. Green light increases it a little more. Yellow light raises it to thirty units. Subject a person to a given color for as little as five minutes, and his mental as well as his muscular activity changes.

The medical profession has long realized that colors can be used to stimulate or depress. Some help people relax and be cheerful. Others stimulate and invigorate them. Still others set up irritation and actual physical discomfort.

Originally developed to increase efficiency in industry, its use has accomplished results in scores of great plants that are truly phenomenal. Testimonials tell how this science reduces workers' eye fatigue, lifts spirits, improves quality and quantity of production. Accidents are reduced.

Its use in hospitals has speeded recovery of patients; effectiveness of medical and nursing staffs has been raised.

In schools concentration is assisted, energy stimulated, eye fatigue retarded among students and teachers alike. Leading hotels have utilized Color Dynamics to import an atmosphere of friendliness, comfort, and good cheer. Offices are made to seem more spacious, pleasing to the eye, contributing to the health and efficiency of employees.

Color Dynamics is in no way an experiment. Its principles have been widely tested in many fields with uniformly beneficial results.

Color can be used as a tool to help us reach our highest potential, and, as we develop a greater self-awareness, we will realize which color or colors will help us the most.

As we progress through our learning experiences on Earth, we develop talents, skills and natural momentums that correspond to the various frequencies of vibration in the seven spheres of color that encircle this planet. In the previous chapter I discussed the colors and qualities of these spheres known as the Seven Rays and explained how these colors and qualities are projected into the physical plane through the seven major chakras of each person. These Seven Rays vibrate not only with different octaves of color and specific qualities, but also with musical tones, fragrances, and natural services or talents.

Our higher selves know what our natural talents are, and we each have the ability to tune in on that information and find out just what we are best suited to do.

We have each volunteered to come into this physical plane to learn our lessons and somehow improve life on this planet. We may not always accomplish that, but it is our original reason for being. What we are to do to improve life on the planet is considered our *Natural Service*. Often, we have totally blocked the awareness of this natural service from our conscious minds, and we need to put forth some real effort to find out what it is.

Frequently, our natural service is referred to as our Divine Plan, and our higher selves are ever striving to assist us in fulfilling our Divine Plan. If you have lost touch with your purpose and reason for being, it is time to go within your heart and reconnect with your higher self. This higher self, your true God Reality, is longing for the opportunity to pull you out of the quagmire of mass consciousness and raise you to the heights of Light Eternal. We have always been told "Ask and you shall receive," "Knock and the door will be open." The time to ask is *now!*

Our reconnection with our higher selves begins with the first heart call. Begin by sitting comfortably in a chair with your arms and legs uncrossed, breathe in deeply, exhale and completely relax.

Gently close your eyes and visualize yourself going within to the "Golden Throne-Room of Your Heart, the Secret Place of the Most High Living God." There you kneel before the altar of Love, offering your all in service as you surrender your human self to your higher self. You then sit upon the Golden Throne, aware that you are perfectly centered, and all of your four lower bodies are in perfect alignment. Through your Heart Flame, the call goes forth:

THROUGH THE POWER OF GOD ANCHORED IN MY HEART, I INVOKE MY HIGHER SELF NOW TO TAKE COMMAND OF MY FOUR LOWER BODIES. GUIDE AND DIRECT ME AND REVEAL TO ME THE FULL GATHERED MOMENTUM OF MY DIVINE PLAN SO THAT I MAY QUICKLY REACH MY HIGHEST POTENTIAL AND BECOME THE MASTER OF MY LIFE, ADDING DAILY AND HOURLY TO THE LIGHT OF THE WORLD AND THE RESTORATION OF THIS PLANET.

After making the call, be silent and quietly listen for the *still small voice within.* After several minutes of silence, ask your higher self to project through your chakras the colors of the Seven Rays, beginning with the Root Chakra at the base of the spine:

Root Chakra	White
Central Chakra	Violet
Solar Plexus Chakra	Ruby-Gold
Heart Chakra	Pink
Throat Chakra	Blue
Third Eye Chakra	Green
Crown Chakra	Yellow

Experience these colors pulsating through each chakra. Now ask your higher self to intensify the Light through the chakra that corresponds to your natural service. Feel that increase of Light and let it register in your conscious mind. Now return your attention to the room, retaining your new awareness.

Remember that no effort is ever lost and even if you feel that you didn't receive any tangible information, your higher self will continue to pour that Light through you until you can grasp it on a conscious level. Persistence is the key. Make the call daily, and, with practice, concentration, and attunement to your higher self, your Divine Plan will be revealed to you as it unfolds step by step.

Once we discover on which of the seven spheres of color we have built our greatest momentum, then we can use this added information as a tool to assist us on to greater accomplishments.

Helene Corinne stated in her book, *Healing and Regeneration Through Color:*

> Light, color and beauty are to be key-words to New Age living. The Aquarian Age is essentially and primarily a color age. Lighter or higher color tones of the spectrum are coming into visibility as, on the one hand, the atmosphere becomes clearer and more attenuated and the ethers more discernible; and, on the other hand, man's sense perception becomes more highly sensitized. With such changes in man and his environment we may expect to lay hold of hitherto undreamed-of powers linked to color radiations. New and amazing developments in the psychology and therapeutics of color are nearing practical application and public use.

Throughout history, the energy of the Seven Rays has been recognized in various forms. In ancient teachings, this influx of Light was called *the pure Love of God.* In more recent times, it has been referred to as *the manna from Heaven,* and now modern science has termed this Light Substance *cosmic rays.*

Scientifically, we know that cosmic rays fall throughout the entire planet at a rate of approximately sixteen times every second. Science knows little about this Light Substance except that it does not originate in the Sun.

In ancient times, initiates taught that this energy contained the divine pattern for all human existence. We are now discovering scientifically that this is an accurate statement. As cosmic rays enter the Earth's atmosphere, they slow down into different frequencies of vibration. The first rays enter the Earth at slightly under the speed of light. Science has determined that these rays carry the Messenger Ribonucleic Acid (MRNA) codes which are the dominating factor in the formula of life. The MRNA codes determine just how the RNA and DNA chains are set up. Therefore, the cosmic rays *do* contain the secret of individual life as we know it. In addition to these first rays that contain the MRNA code, we are discovering that there are myriad other frequencies that we are just beginning to become aware of. Within these other frequencies is the secret of the Seven Rays. Each of the Seven Rays enters the planet on a different frequency, bringing with it its own qualities.

The Seven Rays

The First Ray

The First Ray is blue and includes all of the shades from the most vivid sapphire blues to the softest powder blues. The qualities of this Ray are:

God's Will

Illumined Faith

Power

Protection

Initiative

The essence of this Ray is channeled into the physical realm through the Throat Chakra. If you have built your greatest momentum along this Ray, you would be considered a First Ray person.

Depending on your development, you can be outpicturing the constructive qualities of your Ray, or you can be misqualifying the energy and outpicturing the opposite polarity of your Ray, which would be negative. For example, the natural service of First Ray people tends to make them rulers, government leaders or executives. In the developed person, this can be a service of constructive power and initiative. In the undeveloped person, this can manifest as aggressive human will or domination. By observing the rulers, government leaders and executives, you can easily see whether this First Ray energy is being used constructively as it was intended, or if it is being misqualified by human ego. I want to stress that your natural service does not necessarily mean your job or employment, but rather your natural abilities and talents. For instance, regardless of what type of job you have, you could still be a First Ray person with natural leadership abilities or a Second Ray person with natural teaching abilities, etc.

The Second Ray

The Second Ray is sunshine yellow. The qualities of this Ray are:

Wisdom

Understanding

Illumination

Enlightenment

Mind Force

The essence of this Ray is channeled into the physical realm through the Crown Chakra at the top of the head. If you have built a momentum along this Ray, you would be considered a Second Ray person.

The natural service of Second Ray people tends to be teaching and studying. In the developed person, this can manifest as wisdom and mind force. In the undeveloped person, this can be misqualified into intellectual arrogance or accretion of world knowledge. Again, by observing teachers and students, you can see how this Second Ray energy is being used.

The Third Ray

The Third Ray is pink and includes all shades from the deepest rose to the palest pink. The qualities of this Ray are:

Divine Love

Tolerance

Humanitarianism

The essence of this Ray is channeled into the physical realm through the Heart Chakra. If you have built a momentum along this Ray, you would be considered a Third Ray person.

The natural service of Third Ray people tends to be arbitration and peacemaking. In the developed person, this energy can manifest as love and tolerance. In the undeveloped person, it can be misqualified into superficial love, licentiousness, and lust.

The Fourth Ray

The Fourth Ray is white. The qualities of this Ray are:

Purity

Hope

Selflessness

Perfection

Restoration

Ascension

Artistic Development

The substance of this Ray is channeled into the physical realm through the Root Chakra at the base of the spine. If you have built a momentum along this Ray, you would be considered a Fourth Ray person.

The natural service of Fourth Ray people tends to be art and music. In the developed person, this energy manifests as artistic development. In the undeveloped person, it manifests as Bohemianism or unconventional behavior. I believe the extremes of this energy are more graphic in the musical world than just about anywhere else.

The Fifth Ray

The Fifth Ray is green and includes all shades of green from deep cypress to emerald to pastel shades of mint or sea breeze. The qualities of this Ray are:

Truth

Healing

Concentration

Consecration

Inner Vision

Scientific Development

The essence of this Ray is channeled into the physical realm through the Third Eye Chakra between the eyebrows. If you have built a momentum along this Ray, you would be considered a Fifth Ray person.

The natural service of Fifth Ray people tends to be

medicine, science, and inventing. In the developed person, this energy manifests as scientific development. In the undeveloped person, it manifests as agnosticism or atheistic tendencies. In the field of science, the extremes of this energy are quite evident.

The Sixth Ray

The Sixth Ray is ruby gold and contains all colors from the deepest ruby to the palest gold, including any combination of the two such as orange or peach. The qualities of this Ray are:

Peace

Ministration

Healing

Devotional Worship

The essence of this Ray is channeled into the physical realm through the Solar Plexus Chakra. If you have built a momentum along this Ray, you would be considered a Sixth Ray person.

The natural service of Sixth Ray people tends to make them spiritual leaders, priests, ministers, rabbis, and healers. In the developed person, this Ray manifests as devotional worship. In the undeveloped person, it manifests as religious fanaticism and zealous inclinations.

The Seventh Ray

The Seventh Ray is violet and includes all shades, from the deepest royal purple to the palest lavender. The qualities of the Seventh Ray are:

Transmutation

Forgiveness

Mercy

Compassion

Invocation

Freedom

Ordered Service

The essence of this Ray is channeled into the physical realm through the Central Chakra at the mid-abdomen. If you have built a momentum along this Ray, you would be considered a Seventh Ray person.

The natural service of Seventh Ray people tends to make them adepts, diplomats, mystics, and humanitarians. In the developed person, this Ray manifests as ordered service, culture, and spiritual teachers. In the undeveloped person, it appears as prejudice, snobbery, and prudishness.

To determine what your natural gifts, talents, and momentums of service are, you need to carefully observe yourself. If you will quiet yourself and reverently ask your higher self for illumination on the subject, you will receive the answer. If you will listen to the promptings of your heart, you will be able to experience a magnetic-like pull toward one line of service over another. You should also note how you feel about the various colors and see which ones you have an affinity for. By listening to the *still small voice within* and following your heart promptings and your intuitive feelings, your higher self will gradually lead you to your natural service. Be patient, be still, and be at peace.

The advantage of knowing about the Seven Rays and their corresponding colors and qualities is that now we have another tool we can use to accelerate our self-mastery. Not only can we tune in on the momentum of our natural service to help us reach our highest potential, but, if we want to increase any of the qualities of the Seven Rays in our lives, we can do so by surrounding ourselves with the correct color.

Each color has a specific frequency of vibration and by surrounding ourselves with a certain color, we will magnetize more of the same frequency from the corresponding Ray into our lives.

For example, if we want to increase the vibration of love in our lives, we should surround ourselves with pink clothing or decorate our homes or offices in pink, or meditate and visualize the color pink.

Yellow is the color of wisdom and illumination. Since children are continually in the process of learning, it's a good idea to paint their rooms yellow.

Green is the color of healing. Surgical uniforms throughout the country have been changed from white to green and more and more hospitals are turning up with green walls.

This may seem too simple, but I promise you it works. We have so many wonderful things available to us to make life easier and more enjoyable. It's a shame that we keep ignoring these gifts and persist in doing things the hard way. I don't want you to just take my word for it. Experiment with all of this information, and you will prove these natural laws for yourself.

I am going to conclude this chapter by giving a visualization for each color of the Seven Rays to help you to truly experience the color and magnetize the virtues into your life.

When you are trying to draw the qualities of the Seven Rays into your life, it is important to use vibrant, clear colors. There are many beautiful earth tones and muted colors available, but these dull colors do not have the proper frequency of vibration to magnetize the qualities of the Seven Rays. It is perfectly fine to wear them, and you can even mix and match them with the clear colors, but when you are deliberately striving to increase a particular quality in your life, use only clear colors.

For each of the visualizations, sit comfortably in your chair with your arms and legs uncrossed and your spine as straight as possible. If you would like, softly play some music associated with the color Ray you are going to visualize. A list of that music is included in the chapter on music. If you want to visualize all seven colors at one sitting, you may want to make a tape of your own with six or seven minutes of music for each Ray, recorded one after another in the sequence of your visualization.

Color Meditations

First Ray – Blue

Visualize yourself lying on a beach in the soft blue moonlight. Feel the soft blue Light permeating everything around you. Feel the soft blue waves of the ocean gently wash over you and bathe you in scintillating blue Light. This soft blue essence cleanses your four lower bodies and washes away every trace of anxiety or fear. You feel completely protected and at one with all life.

Second Ray – Yellow

Visualize coming down from above you a sunshine yellow ray of illumination. This electronic Light Substance enters the top of your head and begins to expand through the brain structure, sweeping away the cobwebs of faulty thinking and filling the brain with the yellow essence of illumination, understanding and wisdom. Feel this blazing yellow Light activate the dormant centers of your brain, increasing your ability to learn, to understand, to think and to know.

Third Ray – Pink

Visualize yourself sitting in a beautiful garden surrounded by pink flowers. The fragrance rising into the air from the flowers is a soft pink essence. This soft pink essence of love begins to enfold you in a pink garment of love, and you begin to experience the buoyant joy of pure love. Now visualize that essence of pure pink love flowing forth from your heart center to envelop the entire planet Earth.

Fourth Ray – White

Visualize a crystal white Ray of Light entering the top of your head and descending into your heart center. As this blazing White Light merges with the Spark of Divinity within your heart, it begins to expand like a tremendous starburst out through your four lower bodies, filling every electron of your body with pure White Light. This crystalline White Light begins to purify and restore every cell of your body. Feel the joy of your body as it absorbs this purifying White Light.

Fifth Ray – Green

Visualize yourself in a mountain meadow with green grass and ferns all around you. See the beauty of the healing green trees spread out above you. Feel the green grass below you.

As you lie in the peaceful meadow, experience the healing green energy enter your body. Feel this green essence as it brings your four lower bodies into perfect balance and health, physically, emotionally, mentally and etherically.

Sixth Ray – Ruby Gold

Visualize a brilliant golden robe giving off the radiance of ruby wrapped around your shoulders and enfolding your entire body. Feel the power of this robe as it permeates you with the scintillating golden essence of perfect peace. You feel more at peace than ever before, more calm, more serene. Visualize this golden robe now expanding to engulf the entire planet Earth, bringing a benediction of perfect Peace to all life evolving here.

Seventh Ray – Violet

Visualize blazing up from the heart of the Earth a flame of violet transmuting energy. This flame blazes up through the crust of the Earth, up from below your feet through your four lower bodies. This violet substance transmutes all discordant negative energy manifesting in your physical, etheric, mental or emotional bodies. The Violet Light transmutes all energy back into perfect balance and harmony. Through the power of this Violet Light, you are transformed into a forcefield of transmuting energy, enabling you to transmute all negative energy within your sphere of influence back into harmony and perfection.

The Violet Light now expands forth from you and envelopes the entire planet, raising the consciousness of every man, woman, and child into the realization of their individual responsibility in bringing about the restoration of the Family of Humanity through the abiding presence of Love, Peace, and Truth, the Oneness of All Life.

The Qualities and Natural Service of the Seven Rays

Ray	Quality in Developed Person	Color	Natural Services	Quality in Undeveloped Person
First	Power and initiative	Blue	Government leaders, rulers, executives	Aggressive human will, domination
Second	Wisdom, mind force	Yellow	Teachers, students	Intellectual arrogance, accretion of world knowledge
Third	Love, tolerance, humanitarianism	Pink	Arbitrators, peacemakers	Human love, selfishness, licentiousness
Fourth	Artistic development	Crystal white	Artists, musicians	Bohemianism, unconventional behavior
Fifth	Scientific development	Green	Doctors, inventors, scientists	Agnosticism, atheistic tendencies
Sixth	Devotional worship	Gold and ruby	Priests, ministers, healers, rabbis, spiritual leaders	Religious fanaticism, zealous inclinations
Seventh	Spiritual freedom, ordered service, culture	Violet	Adepts, mystics, diplomats, gentlemen	Prejudice, snobbery, prudishness

Blue	God's Will, Illumined Faith, Protection, Power, Initiative
Yellow	Wisdom, Understanding, Illumination, Enlightenment, Mind Force
Pink	Divine Love, Tolerance, Humanitarianism
White	Purity, Hope, Selflessness, Perfection, Restoration, Artistic Development
Green	Concentration, Consecration, Truth, Healing, Inner Vision, Scientific Development
Ruby/Gold	Healing, Ministration, Peace, Devotional Worship
Violet	Transmutation, Mercy, Compassion, Forgiveness, Invocation, Freedom, Ordered Service

FIGURE 3

10

Music and Harmony

Music is one of the greatest tools we have available to us to assist in maintaining harmony and dispelling discord in our worlds. Simply by playing harmonious music daily in our environment, we are able to raise the vibration of much of the discordant energy that surrounds us and increase the harmony of the planet on a global scale.

Pythagoras taught that music is a sacred science and should be an essential part of each person's training. Music is essential to the plan of creation, for sound contains the very building blocks of physical manifestation. The statement, "In the beginning was the *word*," symbolizes this fact. All physical form has behind it an etheric counterpart, which is the matrix into which the physical molecules are molded. The matrixes of all four lower bodies in the human vehicle are held together and take their form from a musical keynote sounded by the higher self of each person. These notes combine to form a creative chord. Where there is dis-ease of any kind, a lack of harmony is indicated, and by playing harmonious music, the electrons of the four lower bodies can be balanced, and harmony will be restored.

Music will be one of the major healing arts of the New Age. Every sound emanates a certain color and takes on a definite geometric pattern. Every created thing, from plant to solar system, possesses a keynote of its own. The sum total of all these notes makes up what is known as the *"music of the spheres."*

Music is one of the greatest means of bringing our four lower bodies into alignment, and at the same time it expands the harmony of the entire universe. As harmonious music is played, the constructive tonal qualities reverberate out into the atmosphere and literally bathe the shattered, frustrated, discordant vehicles of all life with the essence of pure Light. Humanity is generally bombarded with the destructive vibrations of all of the negative activities that are taking place on the Earth at this time. The more harmonious music that is played into the atmosphere, the more quickly the shadows of discord will be raised into frequencies of perfection.

Harmonious music actually assists in rearranging the electronic substance of our body that has been distorted through misqualified thoughts, words, feelings, and actions. As we move rapidly into the New Age, we will be discovering more and more how effectively we can restore our four lower bodies to vibrations of peace and harmony by using constructive music in our daily lives.

Any music that is constructive will add to the peace and harmony of the planet. Discordant or inharmonious music actually shatters the pole or the matrix of the electrons and causes negative reactions, both in our bodies and in our environment. We have all seen graphic examples of this when a particular note shatters a glass, or, remember the story of Joshua bringing down the walls of Jericho by blowing his trumpet.

Not all music, even if it is harmonious, appeals to everyone, and this has to do with our natural affinities. Any music that is constructive and harmonious is perfectly fine for us to listen to and serves the purpose of adding to the harmony of the planet. There are, however, certain pieces of music available that correspond to the frequencies and keynotes of each of the Seven Rays. By playing these pieces of music we can draw to ourselves the color and qualities of the Rays and increase that specific perfection in our lives. At the end of this chapter I have included a list of music for each of the Seven Rays, so, if you want to draw a particular quality into your life, you can accelerate the process by playing the music that corresponds to the correct Ray.

The question is usually asked, "How is it determined which piece of music corresponds to which Ray?" The answer is that just as there are people living on the planet at the present time that have developed the ability to see higher frequencies of vibration, there are also those who have developed the ability to hear higher frequencies of vibration. This list of music was compiled by people who are able to hear the music of the spheres, and experience the corresponding frequencies of vibration of the Seven Rays in the particular musical piece. Many composers of music have the ability to hear higher frequencies. Some are consciously aware of this, and some are not. This ability is not supernatural or mystical. It is merely a natural part of our development and growth. As we progress we will be developing abilities locked in the unused 90 percent of our brain that we haven't even dreamed of yet. In the near future clairvoyance and clairaudience will be an everyday common occurrence.

Music of the Seven Rays

Music associated with the First Ray radiates through the Throat Chakra drawing power, God's Will, illumined faith, protection, and initiative.

Color: Blue
1. *The Heavens are Telling*, Beethoven
2. *5th Symphony (1st Movement)*, Beethoven
3. *1st Piano Concerto (3rd Movement)*, Beethoven
4. *Adagio in G Minor*, Albinoni
5. *The Warsaw Concerto*, Addinsell
6. *Rose of England*, Novello
7. *Lohengrin (Prelude to Act III)*, Wagner
8. *Believe Me If All Those Endearing Young Charms*

9. *Faust (Soldiers' Chorus)*, Gounod
10. *Pomp & Circumstance #1*, Elgar
11. *Panis Angelicus*, Franck
12. *Enigma (Nimrod, Variations on an Original Theme)*, Elgar
13. *Lohengrin (Bridal Chorus)*, Wagner
14. *The Moldau*, Smetana
15. *Karelia Suite (Intermezzo)*, Sibelius
16. *Church Windows (St. Michael Archangel)*, Respighi
17. *Pomp & Circumstance #4*, Elgar

Music associated with the Second Ray radiates through the Crown Chakra drawing wisdom, illumination, understanding, mind force, and enlightenment.

Color: Yellow

1. *Helios Overture*, Nielsen
2. *6th Symphony (Hymn of Thanksgiving)*, Beethoven
3. *Sadko (Song of India)*, Rimsky-Korsakov
4. *Naughty Marietta (Ah, Sweet Mystery of Life)*, Herbert
5. *Gigue*, Pachebel
6. *Greensleeves*, Traditional
7. *Pictures at an Exhibition (excerpts)*, Moussorgsky-Tomita
8. *Tannhauser (Song to the Evening Star)*, Wagner
9. *Orchestral Suite #3 (Aria)*, Bach
10. *Kashmiri Song*, Finden
11. *Peer Gynt (Dawn)*, Grieg
12. *Carmen (Intermezzo)*, Bizet
13. *The Red Poppy (Scene & Dance with Golden Fingers)*, Gliere
14. *The Invisible City of Kitezh (Forest Scene & Ascent to the Invisible City)*, Rimsky-Korsakov
15. *The Lark Ascending (excerpt)*, Vaughn-Williams
16. *Entrance of the Gods into Valhalla*, Wagner
17. *Air on the G String (Aria)*, Bach

Music associated with the Third Ray radiates through the Heart Chakra drawing divine love, tolerance, and humanitarianism.

Color: Pink

1. *Spartacus (Adagio)*, Khachaturian
2. *2nd Symphony (4th Movement)*, Sibelius
3. *La Marseillaise*, Berlioz and Lisle
4. *Cavalleria Rusticana (The Lord Now Victorious)*, Mascagni
5. *Musette Waltz*, Puccini
6. *Suor Angelica (Intermezzo)*, Puccini
7. *Turtle Dove*, English Folk Song
8. *The Girl with the Flaxen Hair*, Debussy
9. *Rhapsody on a Theme by Paganini (18th Variation)*, Rachmaninoff
10. *2nd Symphony (3rd Movement-Romanze)*, Rachmaninoff
11. *Caprice Viennois*, Kreisler
12. *Piano Concerto #1 (2nd Movement)*, Chopin
13. *Homing*
14. *At Dawning*, Cadman
15. *The Swan*, Saint-Saens
16. *Polovtsian Dance*, Borodin
17. *Carmina Burana (In the Balance-In Trutina)*, Orff

Music associated with the Fourth Ray radiates through the Root Chakra at the base of the spine drawing purity, hope, selflessness, perfection, restoration, and artistic development.

Color: White

1. *Gretchen (2nd Movement)*, Liszt
2. *Parsifal (Prelude to Act I)*, Wagner
3. *Cavalleria Rusticana (Intermezzo)*, Mascagni
4. *Tannhauser (Fest March)*, Wagner
5. *Liebestraum*, Liszt
6. *9th Symphony (3rd Movement)*, Beethoven
7. *Benediction of God in the Solitude*, Liszt
8. *Tristan & Isolde (Love-Death)*, Wagner
9. *Aloha Oe*, Queen Liliuokalani
10. *Aida (Celeste Aida)*, Verde
11. *Sleepers Awake!*, Bach

12. *Entends-tu les Chiens Aboyer?*, Vangelis
13. *Parsifal (Fanfares from the Good Friday Music-Act III)*, Wagner

Music associated with the Fifth Ray radiates through the Third Eye Chakra between the brows drawing in truth, concentration, consecration, inner vision, and scientific development.

Color: Green
1. *Canon in D*, Pachebel
2. *Un Sospiro*, Liszt
3. *Whispering Hope*, Hawthorne
4. *Ave Maria*, Schubert
5. *Moonlight Sonata*, Beethoven
6. *Prelude, Choral and Fugue*, Franck
7. *Toccata and Fugue in D Minor*, Bach
8. *Symphony on a French Mountain Air (3rd Movement)*, D'Indy
9. *Sinfonia Concertante (3rd Movement)*, Mozart
10. *Tannhauser (Overture and Venusberg Music)*, Wagner
11. *L'Elisir d'Amore (Nemorino's Romanza)*, Donizetti
12. *Neratzoula*, Traditional
13. *Piano Concerto #21 in C Major (Andante)*, Mozart
14. *Cello Concerto in C Major*, Haydn
15. *Waltz in A Minor*, Brahms
16. *Pastorale*, Franck
17. *Prelude, Fugue & Variation*, Franck
18. *Chorale in E Major (Conclusion)*, Franck

Music associated with the Sixth Ray radiates through the Solar Plexus Chakra located at the navel drawing peace, ministration, healing, and devotional worship.

Color: Ruby and Gold
1. *Chariots of Fire (entire album)*, Vangelis
2. *Deep River*, American Negro spiritual
3. *The Holy City*, Adams

4. *Chocolate Soldier (My Hero)*, Herbert
5. *Notre Dame (Intermezzo)*, Franz Schmidt
6. *Gymnopedie #3*, Erik Satie
7. *Hansel & Gretel (Children's Prayer)*, Humperdinck
8. *Reverie*, Debussy
9. *Pavane for a Dead Princess*, Ravel
10. *Upon Hearing the First Cuckoo in Spring (excerpt)*, Delius
11. *Orfeo ed Euridice (O Saviour, Hear Me)*, Gluck
12. *Lullabye*, Brahms
13. *Spem in Alium*, Thomas Tallis
14. *Laudi Alla Vergine Maria*, Verdi
15. *2nd Symphony (Primeval Light-4th Movement)*, Mahler
16. *Mass K. 339 (Laudate Dominum)*, Mozart
17. *Piano Concerto (2 excerpts)*, Grieg
18. *Dr. Zhivago (Lara's Theme)*, Maurice Jarre
19. *Aloha Oe*, Queen Liliuokalani
20. *Pater Noster (Amen)*, Tchaikovsky
21. *Incense*, Mike Batt
22. *Fedora (Intermezzo-Act II)*, Giordano
23. *La Traviata (Prelude-Act III)*, Verdi
24. *Joy to the World*, Handel

Music associated with the Seventh Ray radiates through the Central Chakra located mid-abdomen drawing transmutation, freedom, forgiveness, compassion, mercy, ordered service, and culture.

Color: Violet
1. *Nabucco (Va Pensiero)*, Verdi
2. *Symphony #2 (Mysterious Mountain)*, Hovhaness
3. *Die Walkure (Magic Fire Music)*, Wagner
4. *Concierto de Aranjuez (Adagio)*, Rodrigo
5. *Tales from the Vienna Woods (Zither)*, J. Strauss
6. *Die Walkure (Ride of the Valkyries)*, Wagner
7. *In a Monastery Garden*, Ketelbey
8. *Sakura Sakura*, Traditional
9. *Church Windows (St. Gregory the Great)*, Respighi
10. *Symphony #9 (4th Movement)*, Schubert

11. *4th Symphony (1st Movement)*, Schumann
12. *Gaité Parisienne (Overture & Can-Can)*, Offenbach
13. *Arioso*, Bach
14. *Spiral*, Vangelis
15. *The Nutcracker (Trepak)*, Tchaikovsky
16. *Symphony #3 (2nd Movement-Ilya Murometz)*, Gliere
17. *4th Symphony (4th Movement)*, Schumann
18. *Graduation Ball (excerpts)*, J. Strauss
19. *Der Rosenkavalier (Waltzes)*, R. Strauss
20. *Voices of Spring*, J. Strauss
21. *Symphony #7 (Adagio-Finale)*, Bruckner

New Age Music–For balancing and aligning the physical, mental, etheric and emotional bodies.

1. Iasos *Inter-Dimensional Music*
         Crystal Love
         Angels of Comfort
         Helios and Vesta
         Crystal Vista–Video
   Inter-Dimensional Music
   Box 594
   Waldo Pt./Sausalito, CA 94965
2. Aeoliah *Inner Sanctum*
         Celestial Octaves, *Planetary Transformation*
   Celestial Octaves
   P.O. Box 5104
   Mill Valley, CA 94942
3. Ron Dexter *Golden Voyage*
      Tapes I, II, III, IV & V
4. Jordan De La Sierra *Gymnosphere: Song of the Rose*
                  Unity Records
5. *Zamfir* Mercury Records #SRMI-3817
6. Steve Halpern *Spectrum Suite*
7. Vangelis *Chariots of Fire*
   This entire album reverberates with the various frequencies of the essence of *Peace*. If we will all play this music

whenever possible, the planet will be bathed in *Peace*.
> *Tao of Love*
> *Irlande*
> *Cosmos*
> *Entends-tu les Chiens Aboyer?*

8. David Naegele *Temple in the Forest*
9. Mike Rowland *The Fairy Ring, Silver Wings*
10. Constance Denby *Novis Magnificat*
11. Kitaro *Ten Jiku*
> *Silver Cloud*
12. Michel Genest *Crystal Fantasy*
13. Ray Lynch *Deep Breakfast*
14. Jean Michel Jarre *Equinox*

Songs of the New Age:
1. John Denver *It's About Time*
2. Vivian Heart *Songs of the Spirit*
   (Complete tape of New Age Songs)
   The New Age Study of Humanity's Purpose ($9.00)
   P.O. Box 41883
   Tucson, Arizona 85717
3. The New Troubadours *Winds of Birth*
> *Canticle*
> *Homeland*

   Lorian Assoc.
   P.O. Box 1095
   Elgin, Illinois 60120
4. Erik Berglund and Amy Schick *Songs for Peace*
   P.O. Box 0203
   New York, New York 10025
5. Katy Feeny *Sing My Soul*

11

We Are on the Dawn
of a New Age!

Throughout this book, we have discussed the fact that there are natural laws governing this universe, and, by using self-discipline and applying the laws correctly, we can actually take charge of our lives. By now we should have a greater understanding of the power of thought, the advantage of setting goals, the mechanics of creative visualization. We should be aware of the need for prosperity consciousness, the effectiveness of unconditional love, and the responsibility that is ours in restoring and maintaining the health of our bodies. We have also learned that there are invisible energy fields in the body called chakras that we can use to draw more constructive qualities into our lives, and we learned how we can use the gifts of color and music to assist us in reaching our highest potential.

The tremendous upsurge of interest in improving the quality of life and reaching our highest potential is being triggered at this particular time by influences outside of ourselves. We are on the dawn of what is being heralded as the *"Permanent Golden Age."* As we know, in the past, golden ages have come and golden ages have gone, but for the first time *this* golden age is being called permanent. The reason for this is that in ages past a few members of the human race would evolve to great heights and develop the latent powers within. These few people were able to channel constructive energy from the octaves of perfection into the planet effectively enough to sustain an entire area in a vibration of harmony and peace. But, eventually, it was time for these individuals to leave the Earth-plane, and, when they did, the people who were left behind could not sustain the high frequency of perfection and began to falter–thus, the end of that specific golden age.

Now, for the first time in history, mankind en masse has evolved to the point of being able to use the latent powers within and become the masters of their lives. In this Age we are going to realize that, through self-mastery, we can rule our destinies and create an atmosphere of pure uninterrupted Harmony and Joy, literally a "Heaven on Earth." There is not going to be just one avatar, but rather an all-encompassing group avatar that will eventually be composed of every man woman and child living on this planet. Once attaining true self-mastery, humanity will never again be willing to throw itself into the pits of agony, despair, and chaos that we are presently experiencing in our world.

The term "New Age" is beginning to filter into the consciousness of people throughout the planet and is popping up in many different areas. Sometimes it is used almost as a cliche, but there are very real reasons why this vibration is being experienced by so many people at this time. In this context, "Age" is described as a span of time that lasts approximately two thousand years. This span of time is measured astrologically by what is known as the *"Procession of the Equinoxes."* I know at the present time there is a great deal of controversy over the validity of astrology, and I agree that currently there is much human conjecture, error, speculation and even superstition involved in the interpretation of it, but it is naive for us not to acknowledge that, as we move from one major forcefield of energy to another, there are bound to be effects and changes on the Earth. All we have to do is observe what takes place when we have a full moon, or when a sunspot flairs up, or when a comet passes the Earth, or the effects of a solar or lunar eclipse to realize we are *very* affected by every change in the solar system, especially when we move into the energy field of an entirely different constellation.

To explain briefly the Procession of the Equinox, I would like to give you some of the astronomical data. In the heavens there are twelve constellations that comprise what we know as the natural zodiac. These constellations always remain in the same relative position, but because of the motion of the poles of the earth, the sun crosses the equator at a slightly different point each spring. This occurs at the *vernal equinox,* the time in the spring when the days and the nights are of equal length. In astrology this shifting point is considered to be the first degree of Aries. This first degree consequently changes from year to year at a rate of about 50.1 seconds per annum, one degree in 72 years, and one constellation or sign every 2,156 years, completing the circle of twelve signs in about 25,872 years. This is a backward movement and rotates counterclockwise through the heavens. It is this backward movement that is known as the Procession of the Equinox.

As we elevate ourselves in consciousness we will be able to tune in on the true influence the heavenly bodies have on our daily lives, and we will become aware of the far deeper and more complex meaning of Spiritual Astrology. Until such a time, all we really need to understand is that there are specific energy fields associated with the various constellations that definitely affect our lives on this planet.

We are presently moving into the forcefield of Aquarius, and this is one aspect of the term "New Age." Another aspect of the term New Age has to do with the influence of the Seven Rays. As discussed previously in this book, the pure white Light or electronic substance from the heart of the Universal Source of all Life is divided into seven spheres of color as it enters the Earth's atmosphere and bends around the planet. These spheres of color are known as the Seven Rays and for a period of time each Ray in succession has a predominant influence on the planet. The cycle for each Ray lasts approximately 2,000 years, and to complete the revolution of all Seven Rays it takes approximately 14,000 years. Then, as in astrology, the cycle is repeated.

Astrologically, when we come within a 6-degree orb of the next constellation, we begin to feel the influence of the new vibrations. That is what is happening with the forcefield of Aquarius. We have entered within the radius of 6 degrees of Aquarius, but there is much debate among astrologers as to the exact degree. Most agree that we are within 2 degrees to 4 degrees of reaching the cusp.

At this very moment we are also moving out of the frequency of the Sixth Ray and into the frequency of the Seventh Ray. When this occurs, the vibrations of the ending cycle merge with the new and additional gifts, momentums, and qualities of the new Ray begin flowing into the planet on the frequencies of Cosmic Rays. This influx of Light is available to improve life on the planet and accelerate the evolution of all life on the Earth.

The most critical time of any Age is at its inception, and the people living on the planet during that time have a tremendous responsibility to do everything in their power, according to their acceptance and their understanding, to see that these new currents of energy are effectively channeled into the physical plane. Remember that in order for something to manifest in the physical realm, it must be channeled through a physical body. This new frequency of energy is pouring into the planet on Cosmic Rays, but, if we don't absorb it and draw it through our chakra centers, it will not become a physical reality.

The frequency of this Seventh Ray energy is pulsating with all of the perfection of the "Permanent Golden Age." It is violet in color, and has often been referred to as the *"Violet Transmuting Flame."* This energy has the ability to transmute misqualified energy back to a frequency of perfection, and it is vibrating with the qualities of freedom, transmutation, mercy, compassion, invocation, forgiveness, ordered service, and culture. Through these qualities, we are going to transform this planet back into its original perfection and attain our true enlightenment.

This may seem a little too idealistic, but it has been decreed by natural law and prophesied throughout history. The most explicit description of the present hour is in St. John's Revelations, Chapter 10 of *The Holy Bible:*

1. *"And I saw another mighty angel coming down from heaven, clothed with a cloud; and the rainbow of the cloud was upon his head, and his face was as though it were the sun, and his legs as pillars of fire;*

2. *And he had in his hand a little book open; and he set his right foot upon the sea, and his left foot on the land*

3. *And cried with a loud voice as when a lion roars, and when he had cried, seven thunders sounded their voices.*

4. *And when the seven thunders had spoken, I was about to write; but I heard a voice from heaven saying, Seal up those things which the seven thunders uttered, and do not write them.*

5. *And the angel which I saw standing upon the sea and on the land raised his right hand to heaven, and*

6. *Swore by Him who lives forever and ever, who created heaven and the things which are therein, and the Earth and the things which are therein, and the sea and the things which are therein, that there should be no more reckoning of time;*

7. But *in the days of the voice of the* seventh angel, when he shall begin to sound, THE MYSTERY OF GOD WILL BE FULFILLED, *as He has proclaimed to His servants, the prophets."*

The most exciting thing for us to realize is that the "Permanent Golden Age" is already pulsating in total perfection in the etheric realms. It is anxiously awaiting the opportunity to manifest in the physical world of form. It is the responsibility of each and every one of us residing on the planet at this critical time in the Earth's evolution to tune into these frequencies of perfection and draw them into the physical realm through our chakra centers and our thoughts, words, and deeds.

The wonderful part of this is that, since all life is interrelated, we cannot raise one particle of life into a higher state of perfection without improving life for everyone else on the planet as well. Many people at the present time are going through such horrendous things in their lives that they haven't, even for a moment, thought of helping the rest of the planet. We do not all have to have expansive altruistic plans to "save the world," but, if we will just strive to get our own individual lives in order, it will be a great service to everyone.

Once we are truly living in a state of harmony, peace, health, prosperity, and joy, we will automatically become a magnetic forcefield to magnetize the perfection of the Permanent Golden Age into the physical world.

Through self-discipline and self-mastery, we will be raised into a higher consciousness, and consequently help to raise the consciousness of the entire planet. There is truth in the statement, "It is always darkest before the dawn." Light intensifies everything, and this increased influx of Light is pushing all of the negative energy in each person's life to the surface, so that it can quickly be transmuted back to its original state of perfection. By observing the outer world, it is obvious that this is causing extreme imbalances. We must remember the importance of holding our attention on what we want to manifest in this world instead of giving power to the negative things that are constantly bombarding our consciousness through the media and other sources.

Instead of just sitting around and complaining about the world situation or governmental affairs, let's invoke the higher self of every single person associated with the governments of this planet in any way, shape, or form, at national, state, and local levels and ask that illumination and truth pour into the consciousness of each one, to assist all government officials to recognize their responsibilities in bringing forth world peace and restoring the Universal Oneness of Humanity.

We have the ability to invoke the higher self of every person associated with the food supply on this planet and to fill them with the knowledge and method of distributing the limitless abundance of this universe so that world hunger will cease.

We have the ability to magnetize illumination and truth into the consciousness of every person on this planet who is interfering with the rights or freedom of any other person or any other form of life.

Whatever you do, *don't underestimate yourself.* Each and every person is a vital, necessary part of the whole. In any Age there are always the pioneers who must apply the natural laws and gifts of the New Age first to prove to others the truth and reliability of the new energy. We are currently at that precise moment in the Earth's evolution, when those of us who are cognizant of the natural laws begin applying them effectively, so we can be examples of the reality of harmony, peace, love, joy, health, prosperity, and happiness that we know is our natural estate.

We each have a higher self or a super conscious mind that functions only in the octaves of perfection. This higher intelligence of ours is eagerly awaiting the opportunity to take command of our four lower vehicles and guide and direct us along the path of attainment back to the kingdom of harmony within. Through our free will choice, we have chosen, for one reason or another, to withdraw the authority from our higher self and experiment with releasing the thoughts, words and actions of our being through the lower consciousness of our human personality. From this lower consciousness our perspective is not clear, and we get a distorted picture of the Laws of Cause and Effect. Consequently, we have made many mistakes that have resulted in the current chaos in our lives. If we will consciously quiet ourselves and *"go within,"* and deliberately surrender our faulty lower consciousness to the perfect consciousness of our higher self, our higher self then has *permission* to act through us to guide and direct our every action. Not even our own higher self can interfere with our free will, and once we have withdrawn its authority, we must again give it permission to intercede.

As we daily practice this surrender of our lower outer consciousness to our higher self within, we will gradually be able to hear the "still small voice within," and we will discover that the kingdom of harmony within us will be externalized and become a tangible part of our everyday life.

The more adept we become at the application of natural law through self-mastery, the more we will realize our power to transform this planet into a shining orb, Freedom's Holy Star, with no thought of self-acclaim.

The presence of harmony in our lives is just as mechanically explained as the presence of light or sound. It is time to consciously set the pattern of the electronic energy to flow through our vehicles at a frequency of harmony and maintain that frequency throughout the day. Often we think that for energy to be released harmoniously, we must be in a state of meditation, prayer, devotion, or some other type of spiritual aspiration. But in actuality, *all* energy that is released constructively and joyously is a natural expression of harmony. This is true, whether we are cleaning our homes, preparing a meal, working at our jobs, creating a work of art, tending a sick friend, taking out the trash, or performing any so-called menial task. If our attitude is one of peace, love, and joy, our energy will flow forth from us in currents of harmony, adding to the perfection and balance of our own lives as well as to the lives of the rest of the world. Conversely, if we are performing any task, even a sacred devotion, out of a sense of duty, resentment, rebellion, boredom, or even anger or hatred, we are only further adding to the shadows and chaos of our lives. If we will but realize that even the most mundane task can add to our harmony, if done with an attitude of love, peace, and joy, we will see that our hourly living is actually an opportu-

nity to quickly transform our negative energy back into manifestations of peace and harmony. Through practice, we will
become aware that, if we constantly maintain a state of harmony, there will be no set of circumstances or experiences that
can throw us off guard. We will be able to look at occurrences
in our lives objectively and handle them calmly. When we attain that mastery, we will be a Peace Commanding Presence
no matter where we are.

The choice is ours. Our opportunity is at hand.
THE COSMIC MOMENT IS NOW!!!

I would like to share with you a message written by a man
named Fra Giovanni in A.D. 1513 titled "I Salute You!" This
message expresses my heartfelt love for you, and in deep
humility and gratitude, I want to express to you what a sacred
privilege it is for me to be able to walk this planet with you.

I love you, I bless you, and I bow to the Spark of Divinity
blazing in your heart!

I Salute You

Written by Fra Giovanni
A.D. 1513

I Am your friend, and my love for you goes deep. There is nothing I can give you which you have not; but there is much, very much, that, while I cannot give it, you can take. No heaven can come to us unless our hearts find rest in it today. TAKE HEAVEN! No peace lies in the future which is not hidden in this present little instant. TAKE PEACE!

The gloom of the world is but a shadow. Behind it yet within our reach is Joy. There is radiance and glory in the darkness, could we but see; and to See, we have only to Look. I beseech you to Look.

Life is so generous a giver, but we, judging its gifts by their covering, cast them away as ugly or heavy or hard. Remove the covering and you will find beneath it a living splendor, woven of Love, by Wisdom, with Power. Welcome it, grasp it, and you touch the Angel's hand that brings it to you. Everything we call a trial, a sorrow, or a duty; believe me, that Angel's hand is there; the Gift is there and the wonder of an overshadowing Presence. Our joys, too; be not content with them as joys. They, too, conceal diviner Gifts.

Life is so full of Meaning and Purpose, so full of Beauty, beneath its covering, that you will find earth but cloaks your Heaven. Courage them, to claim it; that is all. But Courage you have; and the knowledge that we are pilgrims together, wending through unknown country home.

And so, at this time, I greet you; not quite as the world sends Greetings, but with profound esteem, and with the Prayer that for you, now and forever, the Day breaks, and the shadows flee away.

I would like to close this book by sharing with you a glorious vision of the transformation that is taking place on this planet at the present time.

A very dear friend of mine received this vision during a quiet period of meditation, and she called it "The Vision of the New Genesis."

This perfection is available now and is pulsating in the ethers at this very moment. If we will each offer our four lower vehicles as a cup, a *"Holy Grail"* through which this perfect God Light can flow, we will experience an unprecedented transformation on this Sweet Earth.

Through meditation, visualization, and the buoyant feeling of success, you can be a channel for the Permanent Golden Age into the world of form.

If you feel comfortable doing so, read this vision often, give it the power of your thoughts and feelings and experience for yourself *"The Light of God That Never Fails."*

Vision of the New Genesis

It was a magnificent time! Great changes were taking place all throughout the Planet. Earth was becoming a heaven of wondrous beauty and harmony. Majestic mountains towered above daisy-splattered meadows; jagged peaks soared to pierce the clouds; golden sands of vast deserts flowed toward sky-blue waters. Birds sang. Animals and children played. Men and women lived, loved, and worked together. The sun shone and the rains kissed the ground with sweet blessings.

It was a time of transformation for unto Earth came the dawning of great Illumination. God saw that all nations of the Earth—whatever color, "rich or poor," from East and West, North and South, and of all creeds were sending Emissaries to a sacred Island of consciousness shining in the waters of the majestic sea—to EYNHALLOW—to study together, think together, and care together for the planet and its people; yea, to all life thereon and therein.

And God said, "This is Good." And the morning and the evening were the FIRST DAY of the NEW AGE of PLANET EARTH!

A New World doesn't simply "happen" in outer manifestation. It begins within the heart and mind of each person. God looked at the changes that were taking place and saw that soldiers of peace were separating the combatants of the few quarreling nations. Differences were being resolved through Divine Reason and practical negotiations instead of arms. The leaders of nations were seeing each other, talking to each other, and linking hearts, minds, souls, and strengths for the benefit of all humanity.

And God said, "This is Good." And it was the SECOND DAY of EARTH, the PLANET OF PEACE and GOOD WILL.

The Dreamers—the Souls who are the architects of the World's greatness—were busy. Their futuristic vision lay seeded within the rich consciousness of their adventurous souls. The Dreamers saw not limiting mirages of so-called facts; rather, their vision peered beyond the veils and mists of doubt and uncertainty and pierced the walls of time. God saw the Dreamers at work, and noted that humans were now loving the whole of creation—the stars and suns, the day and night, the fishes and fowl, and all the beings of all the elements. Great joy abounded everywhere. Truly it was a marvelous time!

And God said, "This is Good!" And it was the THIRD DAY of EARTH, the HAPPY PLANET!

God saw that humans were abolishing hunger, disease, ignorance and suffering all over the globe; providing each person with a richer, fulfilling life. Greed was reduced; the wealth and power of the few was no more as understanding brought awareness of the abundance available for everyone. A consciousness of right thinking, feeling and action among the people assured the outpicturing of the DIVINE PLAN for the Planet and its inhabitants.

And God said, "Oh, this is Good!" And it was the FOURTH DAY of EARTH, the PLANET OF DIVINE WILL and JUSTICE!

A flame that burned small within the beingness of each precious progressing soul now grew in size and brilliance. People began to live in harmony with their Father/Mother Home and in peaceful productivity with one another. God saw that the people wisely managed their resources, replaced hatred with love, greed with appreciation, arrogance with humility, division with cooperation, and mistrust with brotherhood.

And God said, "This is very, very Good!" And it was the FIFTH DAY of EARTH, the GOLDEN PLANET.

God then beheld the magnificent Radiance of Restoration. The Emissaries of Light traveled to every land, touched every nation, *blessed ALL people by spreading the word of the perfection of the new GOLDEN AGE. Fragrances of the Light of Truth blossomed wherever their footsteps fell.*

And God said, "Oh, this is Glorious!" And it was the SIXTH DAY of EARTH, the PLANET of GOD ILLUMINATION!

Then, the clarion call sounded as a mighty trumpet to all Great Beings of the Mighty Cosmos, to come and see the miracle taking place. These Great Ones beheld humanity experiencing God Awareness in their lives and on their planetary home. The Great Ones saw, too, the increased GLORY of the ASCENSION FLAME, blazing brilliantly in, through, and around every lifestream! The Human Race served all of life joyously and adopted as their Supreme Law these Truths:

I LOVE THE GREAT UNIVERSE WITH ALL MY BEING— MY HEART, SOUL, MIND AND STRENGTH!

I LOVE THE LAW LIKEWISE, AS THE GREAT LAW LOVES ME!

I LOVE THIS BEAUTIFUL, MIRACULOUS PLANET AND TREAT THIS GREAT BEING WITH INFINITE CARE, AND I LOVE MY BRETHREN IN ALL ELEMENTS OF LIFE WITH THE GREAT UNIVERSAL LOVE THAT IS SO FREELY POURED FORTH TO ME!

The rejoicing was tremendous! The heavens rang with the songs of angels and of men! And it was the SEVENTH DAY of EARTH, the PLANET of GODHOOD!

And God said, "How magnificent You are, O Spirit Sparks! WELCOME HOME!"

RECOMMENDED READING LIST

In my quest for knowledge I have read many wonderful, enlightening books and many books filled with error and untruth. I would like to share with you a few of the enlightening books I thought were fascinating.

Not every word in every book is pure truth, and it is our responsibility to ask our higher self for guidance and illumination so we will have the necessary discernment and perception to absorb only the *"Truth that will set us Free,"* and assist us along the path to our Victorious Accomplishment.

If you come across something that you disagree with, just calmly set it aside and let it go. Don't close your mind and set up blocks by becoming angry, confused, or negative about it.

If your motive for seeking knowledge is *always* to improve life for yourself and the rest of the planet, your higher self will guide you unerringly and will not allow you to be led astray.

Happy reading!!!

Recommended Reading List

1. *The Aquarian Conspiracy*, Marilyn Ferguson
2. *Superlearning*, Shiela Ostrander & Lynn Schroeder
3. *Powers of Your Mind*, Adam Smith
4. *Psycho-Cybernetics*, Maxwell Maltz
5. *Creative Mind*, Ernest Holmes
6. *The Edenburg Lectures on Mental Science*, Thomas Troward
7. *Power Through Constructive Thinking*, Ernest Fox
8. *Spiritual Psychology*, Jim Morningstar, Ph.D.
9. *The Power of Your Subconscious Mind*, Dr. Joseph Murphy, DRS, Ph.D., D.D., L.L.D.
10. *Joy's Way*, W. Brugh Joy, M.D.
11. *The Brain Revolution*, Marilyn Ferguson
12. *The Tao of Physics*, Fritjof Capra
13. *The Medium, the Mystic and the Physicist*, Le Shan
14. *On Personal Power*, Rogers
15. *Toward a Psychology of Being*, Maslow
16. *Beyond Biofeedback*, Elmer and Alyce Green
17. *Stalking the Wild Pendulum*, Itzak Benton
18. *Creative Visualization*, Shakti Gawain
19. *Handbook to Higher Consciousness*, Ken Keyes, Jr.
20. *The Hundredth Monkey*, Ken Keyes, Jr.
21. *The I That Is We*, Richard Moss, M.D.
22. *Love*, Leo Buscaglia
23. *How to Get Control of Your Time and Life*, Lakien

24. *You Are Not The Target*, Laura Huxley
25. *Your Electro-Magnetic Body*
26. *The Path of Action*, Jack Schwarz
27. *The Transparent Self*, Jourard
28. *Man's Search for Himself*, Rollo May
29. *Creative Meditation*, Govinda
30. *How to Control Your Emotions*, Roy Masters
31. *The Perennial Philosophy*, Aldous Huxley
32. *No Boundary*, Ken Wilber
33. *Energy, Ecstasy and Your Seven Vital Chakras*, Gunther
34. *Mandala*, Arguelles
35. *Healing Secret of the Ages*, Catherine Ponder
36. *Occult Medicine Can Save Your Life*, Shealey
37. *Ninety Days to Self Health*, Shealey
38. *Kum Nye Relaxation*, Tarthang Tulku Book 1 & 2
39. *Time Space and Medicine*, Dossey
40. *Getting Well Again*, Simonton
41. *The Therapeutic Touch*, Dolores Krieger
42. *Touch for Health*, John F. Thie, D.C.
43. *Applied Kinesiology*, David S. Walther, D.C.
44. *New Life Through Nutrition*, Sheldon C. Deal, D.C., N.D.
45. *New Life Through Natural Methods*, Sheldon C. Deal, D.C., N.D.
46. *New Mind New Body*, Barbara Brown
47. *The Well Body Book*, Samuels-Bennett
48. *The Gift of Healing*, Worrall
49. *The Healing Mind*, Oyle
50. *Anatomy of an Illness*, Norman Cousins
51. *Dynamic Laws of Healing*, Catherine Ponder
52. *As A Man Thinketh*, James Allen
53. *How to Beat the Aging Game*, Coutoure
54. *Healing and Regeneration Through Color*, Corinne Heline
55. *Healing and Regeneration Through Music*, Corinne Heline
56. *Psychic Self Improvement with Concept Therapy*, William Wolff
57. *The Consciousness of the Atom*, Alice A. Bailey

58. *Thought Power*, Annie Besant
59. *The Only Diet There Is*, Sondra Ray
60. *I Deserve Love*, Sondra Ray
61. *Loving Relationships*, Sondra Ray
62. *The Art of Creation*, Edward Carpenter
63. *Change Your Life Through Love*, Stella Terrill Mann
64. *The Prophet*, Kahlil Gibran
65. *In Tune With the Infinite*, Ralph Waldo Trine
66. *The Man Who Knew*, Ralph Waldo Trine
67. *Three Magic Words*, U.S. Anderson
68. *Children the Challenge*, Rudolf Dreikurs
69. *The Kinship of All Life*, Allen Boone
70. *The Riddle of Consciousness*, Frank Benson
71. *Ye Are Gods*, Annalee Skarin
72. *The Richest Man in Babylon*, George Clason
73. *The Dynamic Laws of Prosperity*, Catherine Ponder
74. *Seed Money in Action*, Jon P. Speller
75. *The Greatest Salesman in the World*, Og Mandino
76. *The Greatest Miracle in the World*, Og Mandino
77. *The Greatest Secret in the World*, Og Mandino
78. *The Gift of Acabar*, Og Mandino and Buddy Kaye
79. *Illusions*, Richard Bach
80. *Jonathan Livingston Seagull*, Richard Bach
81. *There's No Such Place as Far Away*, Richard Bach
82. *Space, Time and Beyond*, Bob Toben
83. *Esoteric Music of Richard Wagner*, Corinne Heline
84. *Beethoven's Nine Symphonies*, Corinne Heline
85. *The Musical Scale and the Scheme of Evolution*, compiled by
    a student of Max Heindel
86. *Varieties of Religious Experiences*, William James
87. *The Impersonal Life*, DeVorss & Co. Publishing
88. *The Way Out*, DeVorss & Co. Publishing
89. *Rays of the Dawn*, Thurman Fleet
90. *The Journey With the Master*, Eva Bell Werber
91. *In His Presence*, Eva Bell Werber
92. *Quiet Talks With the Master*, Eva Bell Werber

93. *The Voice of the Master*, Eva Bell Werber
94. *At the Feet of the Master*, Alcyone
95. *Life and Teachings of the Masters of the Far East*, *Volumes 1-5*, Baird T. Spalding
96. *Healing Stoned*, Julia Lorusso & Joel Glick
97. *Without the Smell of Fire*, Walter C. Lanyon
98. *You Are Greater Than You Know*, Lou Austin
99. *The Initiate*, by His Pupil
100. *The Aquarian Gospel of Jesus the Christ*, Levi
101. *The Masters and the Path*, C. W. Leadbeater
102. *Man: Whence, How and Whither*, Leadbeater & Besant :
103. *Brother of the Third Degree*, Will L. Garver
104. *The Book of Enoch*, Richard Laurence
105. *To Hear the Angels Sing*, Dorothy Maclean
106. *Natives of Eternity*, Flower A. Newhouse
107. *The Kingdom of the Shining Ones*, Flower A. Newhouse
108. *Revelation of the Birth of a New Age*, David Spangler
109. *Vedas*
110. *Bhagavad-Gita*
111. *Upanishads*
112. *Koran*
113. *Book of Dzyon*
114. *Paramartha*
115. *Dnyaneshwari*
116. *Book of Golden Precepts*
117. *Qabbalah*
118. *Secret Doctrine*, Madam Blavatsky
119. *The Voice of Silence*, "H.P.B."
120. *The Secret Teachings of All Ages*, Manly P. Hall
121. *The Rosicrucian Cosmo Conception*, Max Heindel
122. *Unveiled Mysteries*, Godfre Ray King
123. *The Magic Presence*, Godfre Ray King
124. *The "I Am" Discourses*, Ascended Master Saint Germain
125. *The Holy Bible*
126. *The Gnosis and the Law*, Tellis S. Papastavro
127. *The Ascended Masters Write the Book of Life*

Available Tapes

These tapes are specifically designed to help you release and let go of the negative programming that is preventing you from taking control of your life.

1. *"YOU CAN TAKE CHARGE OF YOUR LIFE!"*
   by Patricia Diane Cota-Robles $9.00
   This tape consists of a beginning and an ending guided meditation as well as a lesson to teach the key to self-mastery, the power of thoughts, the process of creative visualization and how to set goals and magnetize the success you deserve into your life.

2. *"UNCONDITIONAL LOVE"*
   by Patricia Diane Cota-Robles $9.00
   This tape consists of a beginning and an ending guided meditation and a lesson to teach you how to use your love as a positive force in your life and transform your relationships into sources of joy.

3. *"THE KEY TO FINANCIAL FREEDOM"*
   by Patricia Diane Cota-Robles $9.00
   This tape consists of a beginning and an ending guided meditation and a lesson to teach you how to open the flow of the limitless abundance of this universe into your life and create for yourself a life of prosperity and financial freedom.

4. *"HEALING"*
   by Patricia Diane Cota-Robles $9.00
   This tape consists of a beginning and an ending guided meditation and a lesson to teach you how to accept respon-

sibility in the healing process of your body and create for yourself a state of vibrant health and peace of mind.

5. *"MAGNETIZING PERFECTION INTO YOUR LIFE THROUGH THE CHAKRA CENTERS"*
   by Patricia Diane Cota-Robles $9.00
   This tape consists of a beginning and an ending guided meditation and a lesson to teach you how to use the chakra centers to draw constructive energy and qualities from the Octaves of Light into your daily life and affairs.

6. *"HARMONY, COLOR AND MUSIC"*
   by Patricia Diane Cota-Robles $9.00
   This tape consists of a beginning and an ending meditation and a lesson to teach you how to use music and color as an effective tool to add to the success and harmony of your life.

7. *"MUSIC OF THE SEVEN RAYS"*
   by Patricia Diane Cota-Robles $9.00
   This tape consists of a brief description of each of the seven segments of music and then is followed by ten minutes of music for each of the Seven Rays. The purpose of this tape is to help you experience the specific vibration of each of the Seven Rays through the corresponding chakra.

8. *"MEDITATIONS TO TRANSFORM YOUR LIFE!"*
   by Patricia Diane Cota-Robles $9.00
   This tape consists of various guided meditations. Side A includes positive meditations and affirmations to help you get in touch with your higher self and establish constructive thinking patterns. Side B includes a visualization to align and balance your chakra centers and a visualization to draw healing Light into every cell and organ of your body to raise the vibration of your body and assist in the healing process.

These tapes are available for $9.00 each or $65.00 for the entire set of eight. You may order them by filling out the following order form or by writing to:

The New Age Study of Humanity's Purpose, Inc.
P.O. Box 41883
Tucson, Arizona 85717

Additional Available Tapes

1. *"CUTTING YOURSELF FREE FROM THE PAIN OF THE PAST THROUGH THE LAW OF FORGIVENESS"*
   by Patricia Diane Cota-Robles $9.00
   It is the forgiver that is FREED in Forgiving. This tape consists of indepth information and exercises using the Law of Forgiveness. At this critical time in the Earth's evolution we are being given unprecedented assistance in transmuting our past through the gift of the Violet Transmuting Flame that comes to us from the Octaves of Perfection. Through this tape you will become familiar with this very effective tool and truly learn how to Love yourself FREE.

2. *"PLANETARY TRANSFORMATION"*
   by Patricia Diane Cota-Robles $9.00
   This tape is being distributed in many countries of the world, and it gives us an opportunity to join energy with many people as we endeavor to transform this Sweet Earth into the perfection that is destined for Her. The tape consists of a guided visualization that enables you to become a Cup, a Holy Grail, through which the Light of God that is Eternally Victorious can pour into the physical world of form. Each time that you listen to this tape and participate in the visualization, the Light pouring through you will first bathe your four lower vehicles and your environment with the beautiful quality of God. Then It will expand to flood the Planet.

3. *"WORLD HEALING TAPE"*
   by Patricia Diane Cota-Robles $3.00
   This tape consists of a visualization designed to balance and purify our four lower vehicles to enable us to be the clearest, most powerful channels of Light we can possibly

be. The purification exercise is followed by the World Healing Mediation that will assist in transforming our Dear Earth into a Star of Peace.

Please make checks payable to **The New Age Study of Humanity's Purpose, Inc.** and include $1.50 for postage and handling for the first tape plus 35¢ for each additional tape.

Additional copies of this book *"TAKE CHARGE OF YOUR LIFE"* may be obtained by writing to the above address also. Please include $8.95 per book and $1.50 postage and handling for the first copy plus 35¢ for each additional copy.

I wish you Love, Success, and Victory in accomplishing your Divine Plan. God Bless and Protect You!

In Light and Love
"I Am,"

Patricia Diane Cota-Robles

ORDER FORM FOR TAPES AND BOOKS

Please send me _____ copies of the book *TAKE CHARGE OF YOUR LIFE.*

I am enclosing a check made out to The New Age Study of Humanity's Purpose, Inc. for $8.95 per book plus $1.50 postage and handling for the first copy and 35¢ for each additional copy.

Please send me the following tapes:
NUMBER
OF COPIES
1. _____ YOU CAN TAKE CHARGE OF YOUR LIFE
2. _____ UNCONDITIONAL LOVE
3. _____ THE KEY TO FINANCIAL FREEDOM
4. _____ HEALING
5. _____ MAGNETIZING PERFECTION INTO YOUR LIFE THROUGH THE CHAKRA CENTERS
6. _____ HARMONY, COLOR AND MUSIC
7. _____ MUSIC OF THE SEVEN RAYS
8. _____ MEDITATIONS TO TRANSFORM YOUR LIFE
9. _____ ENTIRE SET OF EIGHT TAPES

I am enclosing $9.00 per tape or $65.00 for the entire set of eight tapes plus $1.50 postage and handling for the first tape and 35¢ for each additional tape.

Please make check payable to **The New Age Study of Humanity's Purpose, Inc.,** P.O. Box 41883, Tucson, Arizona 85717

NAME _____

ADDRESS _____

CITY _____ STATE _____ ZIP _____

COUNTRY _____

ORDER FORM FOR TAPES AND BOOKS

Please send me _____ copies of the book *TAKE CHARGE OF YOUR LIFE.*

I am enclosing a check made out to The New Age Study of Humanity's Purpose, Inc. for $8.95 per book plus $1.50 postage and handling for the first copy and 35¢ for each additional copy.

Please send me the following tapes:

NUMBER
OF COPIES

1. _____ YOU CAN TAKE CHARGE OF YOUR LIFE
2. _____ UNCONDITIONAL LOVE
3. _____ THE KEY TO FINANCIAL FREEDOM
4. _____ HEALING
5. _____ MAGNETIZING PERFECTION INTO YOUR LIFE THROUGH THE CHAKRA CENTERS
6. _____ HARMONY, COLOR AND MUSIC
7. _____ MUSIC OF THE SEVEN RAYS
8. _____ MEDITATIONS TO TRANSFORM YOUR LIFE
9. _____ ENTIRE SET OF EIGHT TAPES

I am enclosing $9.00 per tape or $65.00 for the entire set of eight tapes plus $1.50 postage and handling for the first tape and 35¢ for each additional tape.

Please make check payable to **The New Age Study of Humanity's Purpose, Inc.,** P.O. Box 41883, Tucson, Arizona 85717

NAME _____

ADDRESS _____

CITY _____ STATE _____ ZIP _____

COUNTRY _____

ORDER FORM FOR TAPES AND BOOKS

Please send me _____ copies of the book *TAKE CHARGE OF YOUR LIFE.*

I am enclosing a check made out to The New Age Study of Humanity's Purpose, Inc. for $8.95 per book plus $1.50 postage and handling for the first copy and 35¢ for each additional copy.

Please send me the following tapes:
   NUMBER
   OF COPIES
1. _____ YOU CAN TAKE CHARGE OF YOUR LIFE
2. _____ UNCONDITIONAL LOVE
3. _____ THE KEY TO FINANCIAL FREEDOM
4. _____ HEALING
5. _____ MAGNETIZING PERFECTION INTO YOUR
                  LIFE THROUGH THE CHAKRA CENTERS
6. _____ HARMONY, COLOR AND MUSIC
7. _____ MUSIC OF THE SEVEN RAYS
8. _____ MEDITATIONS TO TRANSFORM YOUR LIFE
9. _____ ENTIRE SET OF EIGHT TAPES

I am enclosing $9.00 per tape or $65.00 for the entire set of eight tapes plus $1.50 postage and handling for the first tape and 35¢ for each additional tape.

Please make check payable to **The New Age Study of Humanity's Purpose, Inc.,** P.O. Box 41883, Tucson, Arizona 85717

NAME _____

ADDRESS _____

CITY _____ STATE _____ ZIP _____

COUNTRY _____

ORDER FORM FOR TAPES AND BOOKS

Please send me _____ copies of the book *TAKE CHARGE OF YOUR LIFE*.

I am enclosing a check made out to The New Age Study of Humanity's Purpose, Inc. for $8.95 per book plus $1.50 postage and handling for the first copy and 35¢ for each additional copy.

Please send me the following tapes:

NUMBER
OF COPIES

1. _____ YOU CAN TAKE CHARGE OF YOUR LIFE
2. _____ UNCONDITIONAL LOVE
3. _____ THE KEY TO FINANCIAL FREEDOM
4. _____ HEALING
5. _____ MAGNETIZING PERFECTION INTO YOUR LIFE THROUGH THE CHAKRA CENTERS
6. _____ HARMONY, COLOR AND MUSIC
7. _____ MUSIC OF THE SEVEN RAYS
8. _____ MEDITATIONS TO TRANSFORM YOUR LIFE
9. _____ ENTIRE SET OF EIGHT TAPES

I am enclosing $9.00 per tape or $65.00 for the entire set of eight tapes plus $1.50 postage and handling for the first tape and 35¢ for each additional tape.

Please make check payable to **The New Age Study of Humanity's Purpose, Inc.,** P.O. Box 41883, Tucson, Arizona 85717

NAME _____

ADDRESS _____

CITY _____ STATE _____ ZIP _____

COUNTRY _____

ORDER FORM FOR TAPES AND BOOKS

Please send me _____ copies of the book *TAKE CHARGE OF YOUR LIFE.*

I am enclosing a check made out to The New Age Study of Humanity's Purpose, Inc. for $8.95 per book plus $1.50 postage and handling for the first copy and 35¢ for each additional copy.

Please send me the following tapes:
NUMBER
OF COPIES
1. _____ YOU CAN TAKE CHARGE OF YOUR LIFE
2. _____ UNCONDITIONAL LOVE
3. _____ THE KEY TO FINANCIAL FREEDOM
4. _____ HEALING
5. _____ MAGNETIZING PERFECTION INTO YOUR LIFE THROUGH THE CHAKRA CENTERS
6. _____ HARMONY, COLOR AND MUSIC
7. _____ MUSIC OF THE SEVEN RAYS
8. _____ MEDITATIONS TO TRANSFORM YOUR LIFE
9. _____ ENTIRE SET OF EIGHT TAPES

I am enclosing $9.00 per tape or $65.00 for the entire set of eight tapes plus $1.50 postage and handling for the first tape and 35¢ for each additional tape.

Please make check payable to **The New Age Study of Humanity's Purpose, Inc.,** P.O. Box 41883, Tucson, Arizona 85717

NAME _____

ADDRESS _____

CITY _____ STATE _____ ZIP _____

COUNTRY _____